D1337141

One Grump or Two

First published in the United Kingdom in 2008 by
Portico Books
10 Southcombe Street
London
W14 0RA

An imprint of Anova Books Company Ltd

ISBN 9781906032531

A CIP catalogue record for this book is available from the British Library.

10 9 8 7 6 5 4 3 2

Printed and bound by WS Bookwell, Finland

This book can be ordered direct from the publisher.
Contact the marketing department, but try your bookshop first.

www.anovabooks.com

One Grump or Two

The grumpy guide to modern life, from call
centres to getting a decent cup of tea

Arthur Grump

PORTICO

CONTENTS

INTRODUCTION
1

FOOD
3

THE WEEKEND
18

TRANSPORT
34

THE WORKING WEEK
47

POPULAR CULTURE
63

POLITICS
79

TECHNOLOGY
96

SPORT
111

GREAT BRITAIN
125

ABROAD
141

INTRODUCTION

I don't like to complain. I really don't. If the country was in a better state you wouldn't find a more relaxed easygoing chap anywhere in Great Britain. But it's not in a better state, is it? No, it's a bloody hole. A fetid nest of drunks, drug addicts, thieving yobbos and dimwitted psychopaths. And that's just the government. The nation's disappearing round the U-bend and the people in charge are still yanking away at the flush with a bunch of donkey-fanciers and garlic-botherers in Brussels cheering them on. If I had my way I'd string the lot of them up by the goolies for turning a once proud country into a festering boil of car parks and traffic jams, CCTV cameras and government directives telling us to eat up our greens or we'll all die. Where you can get a high-speed internet connection that will pour a torrent of filthy perversion featuring oiled-up midgets into your home, but you'll wait six hours for a bus to the shops. And when you get there every bloody shop is banging out offensive claptrap about bitches with hoes loud enough to make your ears bleed and the shop assistants won't even look at you because they've got some top-level texting to do. Modern Britain, eh?

And that's not to mention the legions of teenage single mums whose legs seem to spring out at right angles from their bodies as soon as they hit puberty and who reckon they've got a God-given right to the contents of my wallet just because they can't be 'bovvered' to shell out a fraction of their pocket money for a pack of prophylactics. Ten years later their kids are all out on the street in their Wayne Rooney football shirts, pissed up on binge

1

and knifing each other while the do-gooders and hand-wringers bleat about how awful it is. Rubbish. Round them all up, I say, give them bigger knives if they love them so much and put them in a big field. Last one standing wins a birching and a ten-year stint in the army. Sounds harsh? Well desperate times call for desperate measures, and just one look at the telly is enough to tell you that these are desperate times indeed. What happened to a nice black-and-white movie during the daytime? Maybe an episode of *The Waltons* or *The Flying Doctors*? These days it's all whiny blubbery chavs with an out-of-control pizza habit who haven't moved from the sofa in a decade except to pop out another baby or microwave another Pot Noodle. The sort of people who buy Jade Goody's autobiography even though they can't actually read because they think it will make them look intellectual.

Where did it all go wrong? Who was responsible for taking a decent British cup of tea off the menu and replacing it with a cup of coffee-flavoured froth? When did all the kids put on ten stone? Why did everyone at work start talking incomprehensible gibberish? And how come nobody ever takes away my rubbish any more? I never agreed to any of it.

No, I don't like to complain, but someone's got to.

FOOD

Coffee Shops

A cup of tea and a nice cream bun. It's a British institution and it's not difficult to get right: some hot water, a tea bag, a splash of milk and a couple of sugars and next to it – on a plate – a cream bun. If you're feeling fancy, maybe a chocolate éclair. Now, I'm not fussy. If you haven't got tea a coffee will do just as nice. Same recipe as above, but substitute the tea bag for a spoonful of Nescafé. I should be so lucky though. These days it's like trying to find the Loch Ness Monster. Oh, you're all right if you want a Hazelnut Mocha-latte-chino or a Half-caff Frappe-bappay-Americano with cinnamon on top or a lemon lapsangsouchong with a bit of bloody *lemon* floating in it or a skinnywhip ooh-la-la with sparklers made with Columbian dancing beans. But try and get a decent cup of tea, made in an urn with PG Tips, and they look at you like you've just blown in from planet Mental.

It's the Americans to blame of course. The bloody septic tanks. They have to muck about with everything. It's the same with cheese on toast. Now there's something you can't muck up, you might think, but show a bit of cheese on toast to an American and five minutes later you've got a deep-pan Super Cheese with extra anchovies and pepperoni. They just can't leave things alone. And being Yanks they can't keep it over

3

their own side of the Atlantic either. No, they think because they invented it, it's better than anyone else's and won't we just be pleased as punch when they ship it over. So one moment you'll be sitting in a nice little café wondering whether to have a sticky bun or an Eccles cake with your cuppa and the next, blam, it's a Starbucks now, the coffee's got ice in it, tea's off and Eccles cakes are now muffins the size of your head. Oh and by the way we're having a really super poetry evening next Friday. Sebastian Arsewipe will be reading his new verses about how we have to respect the Guatemalan folkways.

Bugger that. What about my bloody folkways, eh? You can stick your sunblush tomato and mozzarella panini up where the sun don't shine, just give me back my cup of tea.

Supermarkets

What's so bloody super about them, that's what I want to know? Paininthearsemarkets is more accurate if you ask me. In my day you'd go down the high street to visit the greengrocers, the butchers, the bakers and the fish-mongers. It might have taken a few minutes extra, but you'd get your turbot filleted just the way you liked it and a free whelk thrown in for a regular customer, or your lamb cutlets nicely trimmed with a bit of love and care by a man with three fingers on each hand and a chicken's foot wedged behind his ear for safekeeping. All gone now of course. Your typical high street is a wasteland with a bit of tumbleweed blowing down it.

Maybe a solitary WH Smith clinging on for dear life, but otherwise drained of life by out-of-centre vampire supermarkets.

I hate these places. Soulless, profit-driven, corporate bloody hellholes that they are. What happened to the greengrocer's expertise with friendly prices? What happened to flavour? These days you get veg that might conform to EU standards in appearance, but never-you-mind what it tastes like. Try looking for a decent bit of fish and it's all pre-packaged in a polystyrene tray and trussed up in clingfilm. Same with the meat. Ask where it comes from and what it tastes like and some bum-fluffed sixteen-year-old will scratch his head and look blank, and you just bloody know he's thinking 'Piss off and leave me alone Granddad, I'm hungover.' Cheeky little bugger.

And the trolleys. In my day you had a proper shopping trolley: a big tartan bag on wheels in which you could fit a fortnight's provisions for the Red Army. You wouldn't have seen Coco Chanel dragging one about, but it was functional and best of all it went where you wanted it to, unlike today's shopping trollies. Why make them more difficult to steer the more shopping you've got? Where's the bloody logic? The other day I went in for my weekly shop and with just sixteen crates of lager weighing it down I lost control and ended up crashing into the checkout like a bowling ball. Of course, if there wasn't such a massive queue they wouldn't have needed all those ambulances.

But at least Tesco and Sainsbury and ASDA are trying a little bit these days. (Taste the Difference? So you're admitting the other stuff's inferior then are you?) Try going into an Aldi or Netto or – God forbid – LIDL though and you'll find the dark underbelly of supermarkets. Strange foodstuffs imported from obscure Scandinavian countries and customers that look like they've escaped from some Victorian freakshow lurking at the end of aisles waiting to pounce and bloody *talk to you*. Spine-chilling, that's what it is. No word of a lie, I went into LIDL the other day and right in front of me was a sphinx, an actual sphinx, built from tins of spam. A spam sphinx. I suppose you have to give them marks for trying, but someone in the management office is on bloody drugs if you ask me. And they had a special on. Not a plain old 'three for two' deal on Pantene or a 'buy one get one free' on plastic two-litre bottles of cider like any normal supermarket. Oh no, they had a whole aisle of cut-price incontinence products. Your Tena Lady, your pensioner nappies, every bloody thing you can think of. Disgusting.

Fast Food Restaurants

What's a hamburger when all is said and done? It's just a cheap mince sandwich with a slice of pickle and a splat of ketchup, but the way people queue up you'd think they were putting heroin in those burgers. It's all about the marketing and advertising of course. Open a café on the high street called Mack's Cheap Mince Sandwiches™ with Cold Salty Chips™ and Half-Melted Ice Cream in a Paper Cup™ on the menu and I bet you a hundred quid to a wisp of my navel fluff you wouldn't get half the customers. Call it a Limited Edition Delicio-Burger with Golden Fries and an Ultracreamy Shake though, then splash it about all over the telly, and the punters are breaking the door down and drooling on the counter.

When did *fast* food become a good thing? That's what I want to know. Another meeting I must have missed. I don't want my food fast, I want it cooked right by someone who knows one end of a saucepan from the other and who doesn't have acne bursting into the special sauce every five seconds. If that takes an extra five minutes then I'm quite happy to take a seat here and read the paper. Mind you, we used to have our own fast food in the old days. It was called fish and chips. Fair enough, the British can't cook, but I'll take cod and chips over a burger any day of the week. Not that there are more than two or three chippies left in the entire country these days. David Attenborough should do a programme on them. Those were the days though – a beautiful fillet of pearly white cod coated in fresh batter and cooked to perfection, nestling on a bed of big fat chips, hot and steaming with proper malt vinegar and all served in a copy of yesterday's *Express*.

Oh no, though, the marketing people can't be having with that. Not enough money in it for them. What's a chippy ad going to look like, huh? 'At Rod's Fish and Chips, We Serve Fish … with Chips.' No, instead of good, honest, *tasty* British grub we've got to have plastic seats in the shape of mushrooms, crappy toys that no one wants and limp, pointless, mass-produced food in colourful packaging. At my age you can't afford to be a fan of euthanasia, but for the advertising and marketing blokes I'd gladly make an exception.

Government Guidelines

Five a day this, two units that, just the sniff of an English breakfast will have you in the chemotherapy ward before you can say 'tumour' and red meat's bad for your colon. Well, I'll thank them to keep their noses out of my colon, but if the government wants to do my *spleen* some good they can stop telling me what to bloody eat and drink.

It's no wonder there's so many of these so-called 'eating disorders' around, everyone's so bloody scared of their food they'd rather stick their fingers down their throat than a plate of ham and eggs. Every day you open the paper and it's 'Tests Show Lettuce Makes Your Legs Explode' or 'Jam Roly-Poly to Blame for Necrosis of the Brain'. I'll tell you a true story. I was watching the telly the other day: *This Morning* with Phillip and Fern, I think it was. This woman phoned in beside herself with worry to speak to some celebrity doctor. She was scared that she and her old man were alcoholics because – get this – they *shared a half-bottle of wine* with dinner every evening. And instead of telling the daft cow to get off the line and stop wasting his time, this bloody so-called doctor sympathised with her. I mean, all right, if she's locking herself in the bathroom at 7.30 in the morning and swigging down bottles of Brut then maybe, just maybe, she might want to consider cutting down on the booze a little for the sake of her health, but rehab over a quarter of a bottle of wine? Do me a bloody favour.

It's a bloody liberty, governments poking about in your shopping basket and getting all sniffy because you've got a packet of Viscount biscuits and a nice piece of black pudding. In my day the government was there to run the country, not put the fear of God into anyone who likes a steak with a few beers. Nowadays they don't give a monkey's about making the buses run on time, because they're all too bloody busy lecturing us about stuff that's none of their bloody business. Sinister, that's what it is. The Nazis were the same. It starts with healthy eating and watching your salt intake and next thing you know you're so pumped up on health and efficiency that you think you're the master race and have invaded Poland.

It's this five-a-day twaddle that gets me most worked up though. I mean, do I look like some kind of pallid vegetarian with barely the strength to suck on a Linda McCartney sausage? Of course not. I tell you what, here's a government guideline for you: get on with the bloody job you were elected to do. My colon is not part of your constituency.

Crusading Celebrities

While I'm on the subject, what's with all these so-called 'celebrities' jumping on the health-food bandwagon? That Gillian McKeith woman. For example. What's her game? Going round people's houses and poking around in their poo. I'll repeat that: Poking. Around. In. People's. Poo. What is the faecal matter with that woman? Has the world gone to crap already? You don't give some filthy poo meddler a *television show*, you bang her up in Chokey and throw away the key. I don't care if the entire nation is blubbering over the sides of the bed with whole roast sheep roaming the folds of their fat, you do *not* go fiddling about with human excrement on the telly.

And that Jamie Oliver. Now, I've got nothing against Oliver, so long as he stays in the kitchen where he belongs. Some people will tell you he's an annoying mockney, but the wife's got one of his books and the boy knows his way around a fishfinger buttie, which makes him all right by me. But just because he can put a fishfinger between two slices of bread, he thinks he can go round schools snatching chips off the kiddies? I don't think so, my old mucker. You can bish, bash, bloody bosh all you like, but leave the kiddies their crisps and fizzy pop, OK? I'll tell you Jamie's problem. Just because he grew up over a fancy pub he doesn't realise how much school dinners have improved already. In my day it was Spam Fritters with Boiled Cabbage, Smash and Semolina Pudding to follow, with a skin on it so thick you'd need a pneumatic drill to get through. It was all a lad could do to keep his gorge down of a lunchtime. Chips are bloody gourmet heaven. All right, so a few more of the little ones might be a bit on the tubby side, but let's face it there's always been a porker in every class. Of course in the old days it was no big deal. 'Sweaty' Hopkinson might get a little good-natured ribbing in the showers after PE, but after all he is a ten-year-old boy with a pair of knockers on him like Jordan. Fair's fair. The teasing will do him good. These days it's all hand-wringing and they're not just a bit portly they're 'morbidly obese', but it's all right now because look, Jamie's here with a vanload of cous-cous and an aubergine and tomato bake. A load of nonsense. If you really wanted to get a few pounds off the little chubbers, you'd stop schools selling off the playing fields to property developers and send the lazy toads on a cross-country run. Now *that* would be pukka.

Gordon Ramsay

Mind you, next to this waste of skin the boy Oliver looks like a bloody saint. *Hell's Kitchen, The F Word, Ramsay's Kitchen Nightmares*, they're all the same: an hour of Ramsay swearing at people. What gets me is the gormless idiots just stand there wetting their knickers and mumbling a weak 'Yes, Chef' when he's finished cursing them out. There's me shouting at the telly, 'He's just called you a *************, ****-eating ****** and you're standing there with a frying pan in your hand! Give him a ding round the ear and teach the foul-mouthed sod some manners!' Sometimes you just have to shake your head and wonder what happened to this country. In my day we'd never have stood for it. If some condescending ginger tosser called you a piece of ******** **** because you'd failed to balance a Parmesan curl on top of a wedge of duck-liver terrine with sufficient panache, you'd take him out the back and knock his teeth in for him then jump about on his head until it resembled a flan of summer fruits.

Just once, just bloody once, I'd like to see someone with a bit of spunk wipe the sneer off Ramsay's face.

Organic Farming

This, I just do not get at all. Women in pashminas being followed around the supermarket by kids called Tarquin and Helena making a song and dance about organic vegetables. 'Look love,' you feel like saying, 'it's just a cabbage, fashioned from organic materials. Organic is at the very core of its being. If it wasn't for the organic stuff it wouldn't exist at all. There's nothing about it that is not organic.' But no, they have to have the slightly smaller one at twice the price because it's grown on genuine mud with real slugs trailing about all over it.

Same old story of course. It's not really about the quality of the veg, it's just another way for the middle classes to feel superior. When Tish and Jocasta come round for a bit of grub, Pashmina wants to be able to say, 'Do you want some *organic* butternut squash, darling? It's *organic*. Of course I only buy *organic* these days. Those other vegetables are absolutely full of the most awful things, and one simply can't eat the same food as the economically disadvantaged, can one?'

It's the same people moaning about genetically modified crops. Oh, it's all right for them to have their face pumped with botulism once a month, but try and grow a potato that's resistant to disease and the size of a watermelon so it could feed a family of sixteen and you'd think the sky was falling in. What Pashmina doesn't understand is that if it weren't for chemical pesticides and fertilisers and all the rest of it crop yields would be halved, food prices would rocket and the world's poor would all starve to death. It might be a bit hard on the old greenfly, but unless you want an enraged mob of hungry lower-class types coming round to rummage through your organic fruit bowl, I suggest you don't complain about the nitrates and the phosphates too much.

Farmers' Markets

And so we come to the inevitable companion of organic food – the farmers' market. Popular with the same crowd as above, only this time because they think that buying their pesticide and artificial fertiliser-swamped food from the local peasants makes it somehow all right, like the grub's more 'authentic'. They're being had, of course. If you believe that it's all freshly picked produce and hand-made ethical goodies then you deserve to be ripped off as much as you're going to be. I've often thought that the British people – great in many ways – are right bastards when it comes to making a quick quid and as thick as two short ones when it comes to spotting a scam. It's not a popular observation, that one, and you're probably saying to yourself, 'Hang on there, that's a bit harsh,' but if you want the proof get yourself down to any farmers' market and watch the great British entrepreneur in action.

Look around. What do you see? Blokes in Barbours and flat caps looking grizzled. Of course they're farmers, you only have to look at the weather-beaten faces, plus they're flogging veg out the back of a van or off an old trestle table so that proves it. Then there's a 'specialist' butcher selling traditional sausages made with his own hands to a centuries-old recipe and further down is jolly old Mrs Cake with her home-baked cookies, and so on and so forth.

What a load of rubbish. Answer me this. If the 'farmer' is cutting out the middleman and selling his veg straight to the local consumer, why is it twice the price? I'll tell you why. It's because he nipped into Tesco on the way, bought ten dozen lettuces and smeared some mud on them in the car park. If those sausages are made to a centuries-old recipe why do they taste exactly like Tesco's Finest bangers, only at three times the price? And if those are hand-baked biscuits, Mrs Cake, why have you got a box stuffed with Tesco's, cookie wrappers stashed in the back of your van? Like everything else in the place they're from bloody Tesco's that's why, except now they're a pound each instead of 68p for two dozen, you old fraud.

These aren't bloody farmers, there isn't some time-forgotten hamlet just outside town where the farmer's up at the crack of dawn tending to the pigs while Mrs Cake mixes up her cookie dough as Mother did before her. That's not a 'weather-beaten' face it's the face of a spiv who drives a BMW and downs ten pints a night while laughing about how easy it is to fool people by wearing a flat cap and a Barbour.

Farmer's markets my backside.

Binge Drinking

What young people do to the language these days is a bloody disgrace. When I was a lad 'dogging' meant taking Mortimer out for a walk and a perineum was a type of late-blooming flower. So when I read about binge drinking in the paper my first thought was that 'binge' must be one of these new so-called alcopops, perhaps a combination of the great tastes of beer and minge, but no, it turns out to be something else altogether. Apparently, young people are regularly going into town in the evening and getting blind drunk then fighting, vomiting in the gutter, having sex up the back alley and all sorts of nonsense. Young girls having punch-ups, lads putting too much gel in their hair, everyone swearing all over the shop. It's disgusting. It wouldn't be allowed in the Frugal & Friggitt where I drink. One sign of a youngster making trouble or flashing their chests out and old Mo behind the bar would slam their heads together and kick them round the car park a few times.

Anyway, I won't say I don't like a drink or two of an evening, and sometimes of a lunchtime, and the occasional nip of Scotch in my morning tea, but the difference is I know how to handle it and so do most people of my generation. What young people today need to do is emulate the behaviour of their elders, take a leaf out of our book and conduct themselves with a bit of humourless dignity.

In the meantime I'm going to patent the recipe for 'Binge' – I reckon it could make me a fortune.

Pizza

I have alluded once or twice already to an overall thickening of the girth in the population at large during modern times – a general stoutening or plumpification. In my day citizens were lithe or lissom, skinny or gangly even, but nowadays it seems like everywhere you look it's wall-to-wall flubber: moobs you could use for bouncy castles, great big bums swaddled in tight neon leggings, triple chins a-dangle. Little tiny eyes like dead flies stuck in faces made from half-melted lard. The doctors and politicians will tell you it's down to everything from genes to 'lifestyle' choice, but after literally hours of unrelenting study I can reveal the largest contributing factor to everyone these days being the size of a house: pizza.

I don't remember how pizza crept up on us. At first it infected just a smattering of smart Italian restaurants, but it obviously couldn't be confined. At some point in the seventies it mutated and made the leap into supermarkets. At first nobody thought anything of it, after all it was just a bit of bread dough with tomato paste and some cheese sprinkled on top. Perhaps an olive if it was a posh one. An offering of pizza was an easy tea for the kids and was educational for them to try something a little bit foreign. But over the years, the pizza continued evolving; slowly, but with every new incarnation adding an inch or two to the nation's waistband. First came extra toppings; your pepperoni, salami, different cheeses, and – just to lull you into a false sense of security – pineapple. Then the cunning beggar went deep pan, then even more toppings, this time more confident in their calorie content: ground beef, chicken tikka, cheese, cheese, cheese. By this time it was a menace, people were starting to blob out in a big way, and just when you thought they couldn't possibly squeeze another calorie on they came up with delivery and half the population decided there was no longer any reason to leave the sofa. After getting a delivery menu through the letterbox millions of single young men have never been seen again. If you opened their front door you'd find that their bodies had expanded to fill all available space.

And there it should have ended, but pizza still had one surprise left. The stuffed crust. Who would have thought those pizza peddlers could be so fiendishly clever, so merciless? Now, of course, it's actually possible to watch your thighs billowing outwards while you eat the bloody thing.

THE WEEKEND

DIY

You've all seen the brochures; beautiful glossy photos of what your kitchen could look like at this special low low price, fabulous bathroom suites designed by some poncy designer with huge hair, great ideas to transform your living space ... and it's never been easier with this new extra-durable, easy-lay click-lock laminate flooring, one-coat paint that glides on like magic and non-paint skirting boards that glue on to the wall. Easy? Curse the lying sods. It might be easy for King DIY next door with his ceremonial leather tool belt and shiny royal tools hanging on the garage wall, but for the ordinary citizen DIY leads straight to Olympic-level swearing, despair and penury. And at some point you will *always* acquire at least one major wound.

Your problems will start just outside the DIY superstore. The average family saloon is built to transport a family, not a teetering pile of builders' materials, so you'll have to jam the wife into a footwell and have lengths of two-by-four hanging out of every window. But that's just the start. As soon as you get cracking you'll find that there's something you've forgotten, just a small thing like sugar soap, sandpaper or screws, but you won't be able to make a start without it so you'll have to go back to the DIY superstore, cursing all the way and setting a pattern that will last throughout the project. Then when you start putting down the flooring or gluing on the skirting you'll find you need a specialist tool so back you'll go again. You'll start making mistakes, too. Just a length of wood you've accidentally cut a couple of inches too short, but back you go for another. Then your house will gang up on you. While trying to put a shelf up, you'll find a patch of blown plaster and the whole lot's come down. Back to the DIY superstore. By this time the staff are calling you by name and grinning every time they swipe another fifty quid off your Mastercard. The bills are adding up to the price of a luxury cruise and you're discovering a whole new vocabulary of easy-to-scream swear words.

In the end you'll have a kitchen or bathroom that looks like it was put in by a troop of mentally impaired baboons. The whole thing will have cost three times what it would have if you'd paid Britt Ekland to do it in the nude and you've got a shed full of tools you'll never look at again, divorce is on the cards and you've probably caused some serious structural damage to your house.

The funny thing is that two months later you'll be wandering the aisles of B&Q thinking about building a conservatory …

Gardening

Bloody gardening. It's supposed to be relaxing, but if I had my way I'd concrete over the whole bloody lot and paint it green. Then I might be able to sit back in a deckchair with a beer and the paper and actually enjoy a few seconds of the weekend. But no, the wife likes a bit of foliage outside and so it squats there, green and evil, growing all the time and whispering to me: 'You haven't mowed me in two weeks, what will the neighbours think, you lazy git.' 'I've never been pruned. Not ever. You don't love me.' 'The weeds are choking me. Help me. Help me.'

The weeds are the worst. Well I call them weeds, they're more like triffids really. Great ugly brutes that grow in seconds, migrate across the garden at the speed of light and have the root systems of a giant redwood. I can spend all day carefully pulling them out of my herbaceous border, turn my back for five seconds for a well-deserved cuppa, and they're all back, leering at me. Only this time they've brought their stinging nettle mates. If I totted it all up I've probably spent the best three years of my life – the weekend years – kneeling in soggy mud fighting a losing battle against bindweed. I wouldn't mind so much, but when I do eventually clear a space and stick a couple of geraniums in they're always dead within a week. Anything spiky, ugly or poisonous will grow like topsy, but stick something in the ground that you've paid money for and you'd think it was the Gobi Desert out there.

I wouldn't mind so much if the missus gave me a hand now and again. Oh, she'll come out occasionally. If it's sunny. With a straw bonnet and a pair of secateurs. And she'll wander up and down humming and snipping at this and that – making no real difference of course, but happy to be giving something the snip – then go back in the house leaving behind sixteen piles of vicious, thorny vegetation, each one of which looks as though it's got a sleeping castle at its centre. If I'm feeling brave I might mention that perhaps she could clear them up, but all I ever get in response is a wide-eyed look of wonder that she could possibly have married a man so lacking in chivalry as to expect her to tidy up her own bloody mess. So while everyone else is sipping gin and tonic in miraculously well-manicured garden which seem to require no maintenance whatsoever, I'll be fighting a ton of razor-wire vegetation into the boot of the car to take to the tip.

Which, I'm sure you'll agree, is a *great* way to spend the weekend.

The Tip

And speaking of the tip. Why is it that no matter how many times you go, it's never enough? You can clear out the shed from now until the end of time and just when you think you're finished it will spawn another load of old crap that the bin-men will refuse. I suspect that the neighbours, in an effort to avoid the bloody tip, are sneaking into the garden in the night and throwing their rubbish in my shed. And who can blame them? I mean, what don't the binmen refuse these days? Fill the wheely bin full of fifty-pound notes and bottles of champagne and they'd get all sniffy and tell you that paper and glass waste need to go to the tip.

We used to have dumps in the old days. You could just drive the car in and dump whatever you liked, hence the name, you see? But now, thanks to the beardie yoghurt munchers we've got to *preserve* the environment, which means recycling, which means going through each and every sackful of rubbish and sorting it into the right receptacle, which means it takes an hour, and guess what? Hey presto there's a three-hour tailback just to get to the bloody tip to drop off two sacks of the wife's snippings and an old coffee table I've never seen before in my life.

Bank Holidays

Bank holidays? Useless holidays, I call them. Little crumbs of respite that you look forward to for weeks, then blink and you've missed them. Just enough time to put up a shelf and watch a crappy Roger Moore Bond movie then it's back to work. Abolish all bank holidays, I say. Not an immediately popular idea I'll grant you, but ask yourself this: would you rather be forced to take a single day now and again when it's guaranteed to be weeing down with rain, all the roads are gridlocked, Homebase is packed to the rafters with a million other poor saps who've also been told to put shelves up, everywhere else is closed and what good is a single day to anyone, really? *Or* would you rather roll them all together and have an extra two weeks to take off whenever you felt like it?

I mean, what are they for exactly? New Year's Day? I've got the hangover from hell and I'm not going to enjoy the day anyway, so I might as well go into work and be miserable there. May Day? I think you'll find that the days of sweet young virgins dancing round a maypole to ensure a bountiful harvest are long gone. These days if you can find a virgin at all, which I seriously doubt, they're more likely to be knocking back the Superbrew and happy- slapping someone. So that's another one down. Christmas? Easter? Don't make me laugh. There's not a church in the land with more than one worshipper and she died years ago, they just haven't bothered shifting her off the pew. In case you hadn't noticed we're a la-di-da secular multi-cultural society now and the Jews, Muslims, Hindus, Pagans, Jedis, etc. couldn't give a vicar's tinkle about Easter and Christmas. Besides, if you've got a few days serious church-going pencilled in, you can always take it out of your new two-week holiday. August Bank Holiday? How about August fortnight holiday? How about not going into work for the *whole* of August and still having ten days' holiday time left?

Bank holidays are a rip-off. Frankly I don't want a day off in April staring out the window at sheets of rain just for the sake of some mouldy old tradition. I'd rather go into work and have an extra two weeks on the Costa Brava thankyouverymuch.

The Weather

And talking about the weather, what happened to global warming? I was looking forward to that. Even left the motor running in the drive so that it could pump out a few more greenhouse gases. While all these so-called scientists were wringing their hands and bleating on about the catastrophe of climate change, I was down B&Q getting a new patio set. Those Mediterranean countries have been getting the best of it for ages, I thought. It's about time we have a go and, frankly, the loss of a polar icecap or two, East Anglia slipping beneath the waves and a few dangly moles on the face is a price well worth paying.

I should have known, of course, that the British weather is made of sterner stuff. It'll take more than a few carbon emissions to shift the masses of grey cloud lurking above that we all know and hate. Especially at the weekend. Not even the vindictive gods that control Britain's weather can quite manage 365 consecutive overcast days or torrential rain *every* year, but they can make sure that the sun only ever shines between Monday and Friday (bank holidays excepted) when you're sweltering in some hessian cubicle without even a window to look out of.

The Pub

You wouldn't stick the Queen – God bless her – on *Extreme Makeover*, would you? All right, you might take fifty years off her with a spot of lipo, a facelift and a chest enhancement, but that's not the point. Some things are sacrosanct; you just do not muck about with them, and as far as I'm concerned pubs fall into the same category as her maj.

But try telling that to today's pub managers and marketing people. According to them the traditional old boozer that hasn't changed since the thirteenth century looks tired and out of date and needs to appeal to today's younger, more style-conscious drinker. They'll be leafing through the Reproduction Tat, Inc. catalogue and buying large oars, genuine fifties-style neon signage, hand-aged wood-effect beer barrels, bookcases moulded and painted to look just like there's actual books in, gramophones made in China, fishing nets and much, much more. But even that won't be enough for them. Once they've got going your historic public house that has been serving the community for centuries will suddenly become a theme pub. What a great idea. You're in Norwich, but they'll make it an *Irish* theme pub and take down the King's Arms sign – it doesn't matter that the pub was so-named because Charles I stopped there to enjoy a pint – and rebrand everything. Now it's called O'Buggery's. There will be O'Buggery's plastic bunting everywhere, with a shamrock on for authenticity, and they'll nail an almost antique bodhrán to the wall. Local beers have been replaced by Guinness and alcopops, and the Suffolk ham the farmer down the road hand-cures is now off the menu and instead you can get Colcannon and Dublin Bay prawns that they pick up in Iceland and microwave.

Just when you think it can't get any worse, they'll realise there's still some of the original atmosphere left and install a big-screen TV, which will be left on *all the time,* so that punters who might have come in for a chat with their mates can now have their conversation drowned out by *EastEnders* and will sit gawping at the screen all night …

Well, if that's what today's younger, more style-conscious punter demands then in my humble opinion they can sit out in the car with a bag of crisps and a Coke until they've learned some bloody sense.

Karaoke

It's a little-known fact that karaoke began as a form of torture during World War II. Prisoners of war would be marched into a hall and forced to listen to the camp commandant wail his way through 'Sorry Seems To Be The Hardest Word' and 'My Way', which is why all those liberated soldiers on VJ day look so haggard. A lot of the poor beggars didn't make it. By the time the war ended, it was too late. The Japanese had got a taste for inflicting karaoke on people and the disease began to spread.

Don't get me wrong, I've got nothing against a bit of pub entertainment, I'm quite happy for 'Arthritic' Dave Spandex to provide some ambience by bashing out John Denver hits on his organ quietly in the corner. He's a seasoned professional who used to work Butlins and has his own gold lamé jacket. However, inviting a roomful of pissed-up Saturday-night revellers to belt out 'Bohemian Rhapsody' and 'You're The One That I Want' is to human dignity what a chainsaw is to head massage.

It'll start low-key. Everyone will be nudging each other and saying, 'You do it, no you do it,' then somewhere around the third pint a lass will get up and titter her way through 'I Will Always Love You'. This is the time to leave, for the floodgates are now open and around the sixth pint you'll find your self-respect has deserted you and you'll be up on stage clutching your drink and doing your own special version of 'House of The Rising Sun' with all the tuneful notes removed. And that's it, you've had a taste of it now, a taste of the spotlight, a taste of *stardom*. At first you'll pass the microphone on happily, but then you'll find you're sitting on your stool chafing for it to be your go again. Now you've had eight pints and a bit of practice you're loosened up, and next time you'll wow them. And so, by the tenth pint you'll be on your knees with your shirt open to the waist and your hairy gut hanging out. In your head you're Rod Stewart in his seventies heyday, but to everyone else your version of 'If You Think I'm Sexy' sounds like the screeching of a troop of drunken otters. Nobody's getting that mike off you now though, dammit. You're Tom Jones, Freddie Mercury and Frank Sinatra all rolled up in one. What serious music fan would want you to stop singing, especially now you're just about to start on 'Wild Thing'?

In the end the bouncers will pull you off the stage, of course, and bundle you out the door kicking and still screaming 'Wild thing, I think ah luuuurve you, but I gotta know fo' sure,' and in the morning you'll realise that you can never go back to that pub again. The trouble is, they've all got karaoke machines now.

Shopping Centres

What I really want to see in a shopping centre is a pistol shop, so I can shoot myself in the head rather than lug bags and bags full of crap around some muzak-playing hellhole all day. But no, they won't let the mugs, sorry 'customers,' take the easy way out. Shopping is now Britain's favourite pastime so you'll just have to spend your weekend being jostled round Tie Rack and Knickerbox like all the other brand-obsessed, advert-anaesthetised lemmings, buying rubbish you don't really want or need at prices that would make Rockefeller weep.

Oh, they've got it all worked out, the retailers. People aren't interested in the goods these days, they want the whole 'purchasing experience', which basically means that the less there is in a shop the more expensive it is. You go into some of these places and there's one pair of jeans on a podium, artfully arranged in architecturally designed surroundings and guarded by ten shop assistants, all of whom look like they just stepped out of a perfume advert. Never mind that you could get a pair of perfectly serviceable George jeans in ASDA for a tenner, probably turned out of the same Chinese sweat-shop, these have an *Armanucci Smith* label on, so they're 350 quid. Well, here's a little secret for anyone who's bought a pair of jeans for 350 quid. Are you ready? Here we go. No pair of jeans is worth 350 quid. No, not even if Armanucci Smith personally hand-tailors them for you from denim woven by angels on golden looms. Basically – and I shouldn't have to explain this – you paid a fiver for the jeans and the rest of it goes on paying architects and beautiful staff who are specially trained to sneer at you, because while you may be a Nobel Peace Prize winner and they just work in a shop, you'll never, ever be as cool as them no matter how many pairs of £350 jeans you buy. You've been had. Armanucci Smith is wetting himself laughing all the way to George at ASDA.

Shopping centres are there for one reason and one reason only, to fleece you like you've never been fleeced before. They are the modern equivalent of Dick Turpin, only the marketing and advertising people have now worked out how to make you line up willingly to be robbed. Why else would otherwise perfectly sensible people spend the weekend straining through the crowds under the weight of seventeen bags while spending an entire year's wages in one day? With not even a toilet in sight. Just remember, next time you feel like a trip to the local shopping centre; shopping is not a pastime, it's a chore. Now have a cup of tea and a peaceful sit-down in those favourite old jeans that still have a bit more wear in them. Isn't that better?

The Gym

So, I'm not as young as I used to be and I have to admit the pecs aren't perky, the old six-pack is now a one-pack, and the backside is sagging like two sacks of semolina pudding. Everyone's banging on about taking healthy exercise and apparently lifting an iron-laden Guinness does not count. There are two options – jogging round the park, or weekends at the gym. Now you have to weigh up the pros and cons very carefully, and your thinking will run along these lines:

THE PARK

Pros
It's free

Cons
It will be raining 90 per cent of the time
Gobby teenagers will point and jeer and throw stuff
Dog crap
Cottaging

THE GYM

Pros
Nubile young women in tight gym gear bouncing away on the treadmills
Nubile young women in bikinis in the jacuzzi and sauna
Nubile young personal trainers
Nubile young masseuses running their hands over your body

Cons
For the same price you could just have a tummy tuck, pec implants and a butt lift

Seems like an easy decision, doesn't it? It's a bit pricey, but it's warm and dry, the changing rooms are scented with lavender, they let you steal the towels and they even have a dinky little café. And let's not forget the nubile young women in the tight gym gear. But take my advice, do not go to the gym. No matter how many yobbos are cursing at you in the park, whatever hurricane you have to brave while treading in poo at every step, not even if

George Michael himself is lurking in the trees. Just don't do it. Oh, you'll sell a kidney to join Cannon's Place and it will all seem very nice at first – the fluffy towels, the sumptuous changing facilities, the helpful, friendly staff, but then you'll look around and realise that you've made a dreadful mistake, for the gym is not for people who want to *get* fit, it's for people who already *are* fit. Posing body nazis who look like they were chiselled out of stone by Michelangelo, glowing Adonises and sylph-like beauties with not a fat cell to share between them. You – in comparison – look like you not only ate all the pies but made a good start on the sausage rolls too. You couldn't be more out of place if the gym was on a frozen gas planet and all the other members were spiny ice creatures. You'll puff and pant and sweat all right, but only because they made you sign up for a year in advance; you'll go purple and make all the gruesome faces in the world as you strain for that last bench press. But you'll never ever look like the beautiful people and every time you go a little bit more of your self-esteem will evaporate.

Believe me, getting hit in the head by a bottle of cider in the pouring rain is the better option.

Dinner Parties

In the old days you'd get a keg of Watney's Party Seven, a couple of bottles of sparkly white plonk for the ladies and tip a packet of Salt 'n' Vinegar Discos into a bowl. If it was a special occasion you might go to the effort of a few chipolatas or some cheese and pineapple on sticks. And there you had it: a party. Oh, it could get a bit debauched. A few drinks and everyone would be doing the conga round the house and passing balloons around with their knees, but we knew how to enjoy ourselves in those days. That's not good enough any more, though. Letting your hair down with a few mates is too easy. Instead we've got to have bloody dinner parties. We've got to showcase our culinary skills and spend the evening making polite conversation over a 'rather special rosé with notes of elderflower and cat jasmine' while listening to some noodling jazz – or worse still, bloody classical. It's not about having a laugh, it's about lifestyle. Like we all live in a bloody Habitat advert.

The truth is, British people can't cook. Well-known fact. For all we like to watch people chucking crepes around on the telly or flambéing a spatchcocked goat, anything beyond ham, egg and chips is just a fantasy. The French cook, the Brits drink. It's just the way it is. Invite any French bloke down the pub for ten pints of Dog Bolter and watch what happens. He won't be able to manage it. It'll be a horrible mess. And the same is true of British people in the kitchen.

But no, everyone's been out and bought Jamie Oliver's latest book and are now desperate to show the neighbours what fancy olive oils they are using on everything. This, in actuality, means they spent the entire day sourcing ridiculously over-priced fancy ingredients and making sure all the glasses are the right shape, choosing the right wines to go with the chicken, screeching around the kitchen which is billowing smoke all over the place and then you sit in cringing embarrassment when they serve up a tower of avocado terrine and smoked salmon mouse that looks as if some jihadi's driven a plane into it.

Well, I for one am rebelling. The wife can have her dinner parties, but I'll be headbanging to Slade in the other room with a chicken leg, a party hat, a balloon wedged in my flies and a six-pack of Tennents. We'll see who has a better time, eh?

Transport

Speed Cameras

Now, I may not be a young man any more, but I know how to handle a motor. Some of these 'boy racers' you see cruising the high streets these days have had more collisions just getting out of bed in the morning than I've ever had (though not the wife), but even so is it any reason to penalise the rest of us with these bloody speed cameras?

Not that it's about safety. I wouldn't mind so much if they just put them on so-called accident blackspots where old ladies were prone to being mown down by young Stirling Mosses behind the wheel of a souped-up Astra. No, it's all about the economy, stupid. Speed cameras are now worth more in revenue to the government than Inheritance Tax and Window Tax combined. No word of a lie, the money they make from speed cameras paid for the last three wars. I could show you the paperwork.

Think about it. Where do they put the most speed cameras? In heavily built-up areas where they're bound to collect the most dosh, that's where. Mum's just picked up the kids from school, Dad's on the way home and dinner's not in the oven. It's only natural that she'll scream out of the school gates doing a ton. Flash, that's another sixty quid thankyouverymuch. Late getting to the office and the traffic's miraculously cleared on the

High Street? What normal person wouldn't put their foot down? Flash. Closing time at the pub and you and your mates fancy a burn on the way home? For crying out loud, all the kiddies are in bed, it's a harmless bit of fun. But no. Flash, flash, flash, that's the final payment on the Trident upgrade sorted.

Of course, you can choose to pay the fine *or* you can opt to spend a day on an 'Awareness Course' where some sandal-wearing beardie bleats on about the rights of pedestrians. Give me strength. Do pedestrians pay road tax? No, of course not. Stands to reason that my tax paid for it so I get priority. What about the rights of motorists? What about awareness of how bloody infuriating speed cameras are? Bring back plod with the speed gun that's what I say. So you get caught doing ninety in a residential area? Slip him a tenner. He's happy, you're happy and no one's the wiser.

Traffic Calming Measures

Speed bumps? There's a misnomer if ever there was one. I tried hitting one at seventy and got no extra boost of speed off it at all. If anything it slowed me right down. It's not easy to maintain a decent whack when your suspension's dragging along underneath the motor. I wrote to my MP of course, but got no reply whatsoever. All I got was a bloody great bill from the garage and a slipped disc in the neck when my head hit the car roof.

Traffic Wardens

'If two traffic wardens were drowning, and you could only save one of them, would you go to lunch or read the paper?'

Ah, they come in for some stick though the old traffic wardens, don't they? You hear some stories. People spitting on them, kicking them. The verbal abuse would curl your ears up. All perfectly fair and above board in my opinion. Jumped-up little Hitlers with their notebooks and walkie-talkies. Heartless, vindictive bloodsuckers. If I had my way the whole lot of them would be clamped. Both legs. You could throw away the key, too, for all I care.

Roadworks and Traffic Jams

If there's one thing that's guaranteed to raise the pressure to the point where blood's squirting out my ears it's traffic jams. Every time I get in the motor it's the same story: six bloody hours sitting motionless with nothing to do but curse and listen to some ghastly play about a knitting club on Radio Four.

Usually it's roadworks, of course. Gas pipes leaking, water mains burst, potholes, subsidence, extra lanes; it all boils down to shoddy workmanship in the first place. And who suffers? The decent, hard-working motorist, as usual. It's estimated that there are about 40 million cars in the UK. On top of car tax (at an average of £150 per vehicle that's £6 billion a year) we have to pay 75 per cent tax on petrol. If half of the cars in Britain use a litre of petrol a day it works out to roughly about £5 billion in fuel tax. So, that's about £11 billion a year give or take the odd penny. With £11 billion to play with every bloody year you'd have thought they could build a road that wouldn't need digging up every five minutes, wouldn't you? If the *Romans* could build a road that lasted a millennium with nothing more than some sticks and pebbles, why are they patching up the A41 every five minutes? One thing you never saw in Roman Britain was traffic reduced to one lane with a thirty-mile tailback of charioteers, all having to wee in bottles and tip it out the side. And I'll tell you why. The Romans weren't afraid to gee up the workers with a touch of the lash every now and then. A work ethic that did them proud. What do you get these days? Cones and flashing lights all over the shop and a solitary fat bloke leaning on a shovel and slurping a cup of tea down him as if there's all the time in the world. Meanwhile your backside's gone numb, you're on the way to deep-vein thrombosis and to top it all it's time for *Woman's Hour*.

It's not all roadworks of course. Quite often some selfish beggar's had a blowout at eighty-five, slammed into the central reservation and caused a pile-up. The end result is the same though: signs everywhere saying 'maximum speed thirty' and the dog's died of heat exhaustion on the back seat. I wouldn't mind so much, but they're taking the piss with that maximum speed business. Six hours I was on the M6 the other day and in all that time I moved half an inch. There's snails overtaking me on the inside lane, and above my head a flashing sign going 'maximum speed thirty'. I'm desperate for a pee and am running out of swear words with every flash. What wouldn't I give to be doing thirty? Thirty miles an hour's a motoring paradise. But no, thirty's just a dream. In the real world you're red-faced with fury, watching the heat haze rising off the tarmac and there's nothing you can do except get the bottle out again and wonder whether it's time to start eating the dog.

The School Run

And another thing. Why the bloody hell can't the kiddies walk to school these days? Try and get anywhere between 8.00 am and 10.00, or 3.00 pm and 5.00 and it's bumper-to-bumper people movers and four-by-fours with sticky brats making faces at you out the windows of every motor in sight. I wouldn't mind so much, but it's not as though they don't need the exercise. No, I'm sorry, but I've got an urgent appointment at the bookmakers and little Johnny's looking like Jabba the Hut. A five-mile hike in the sleet twice a day would do him the power of good, so stop being selfish, get off the road and let adults use it. Do I come round and play on Johnny's PlayStation? No. So he can get off my bloody road.

Laziness, that's what it is, sheer un-bloody-believable laziness. Try and suggest that to one of these mum's though and all you hear is, 'Oh he can't walk that far.' And why not? Because the idle little beggar's spent so long sitting in front of computer games that his legs have atrophied. He's got less muscle on him than a butcher's pencil and he thinks that walking is something they used to do in the Dark Ages before in-car DVD players were invented. Is it any wonder this country's in the state it's in?

And Heaven forbid you have to pass an actual school. Total gridlock. These mums use the road as a bloody car park and there's nippers running everywhere. Try and nudge them gently out of the way with your bumper and they treat *you* like a criminal, never mind the fact that some 'yummy' mummy's Land Rover Discovery is triple parked while she's having a gossip with her mates!

If you do finally get moving, chances are some gurning lollipop bastard in a white coat's going to jump out at you with a sign saying 'STOP CHILDREN'. How bloody right they are if only they knew. Stop Children. There's too bloody many of them and they're clogging up the highways.

Takeaway Delivery Mopeds

And talking about laziness, what's all this about? Call me old-fashioned, but in my book if you want a nice piece of halibut and chips with a pickled egg you get off your backside, onto shanks's pony and stroll down the road. A gentle amble sharpens the appetite and you get to chat with Roger and Doris behind the counter while they wrap up your order for you to *take it away*. The clue's in the bloody name, you see?

But no, that's not good enough for youngsters today. Oh no. You'd think being prised off the sofa was in contravention of the European Bill of Human Rights. They have to have their takeaway food *delivered*. Ooh la de da, we can't expect little Lord Fauntleroy to stop playing *Grand Theft Auto* for five minutes and squeeze his massive arse out the door now can we? That two-minute walk to the curry house or the pizza place is *such* an inconvenience when you've got *such* important things to do. No, instead Raj or Guiseppe have got to bring it to him. And he probably doesn't tip the poor beggars.

What really bothers me about it though, really, really sticks in my craw is that the direct consequence of these bone-idle little gits not being able to drag themselves any further than the telephone is that I've got bloody delivery mopeds buzzing around the motor like wasps every time I leave the house. Every single one of them has an 'L' plate dangling off the back, and all of them are on a mission to get back in the warm as quickly as possible. Roughly translated, this means 'I haven't got the faintest idea what I'm doing but I'm going to act like I own the road anyway.' You see them whizzing about like Evel Knievel on a hairdryer and for what? Minimum wage and all the stuffed crust you can eat? Sorry, my friend, but if you're going to cut me up you've got to have a much better reason that that. They've got no consideration whatsoever for other road users or regard for their own personal safety, which is just as well because if one gets in my way I'm making no concessions whatsoever.

Trains

I'm an easy-going bloke as a rule, but the bloody railways make me fume. You can forget putting your feet up for a peaceful game of chess like in the adverts, it's like the Battle of the bloomin' Somme all over again, except three hours late and covered in old chewing gum.

Years ago a train journey was a treat. You'd start your journey in a chocolate-box station with flowers every-where, home-made cheese sandwiches with the edges only slightly curled up and tea in a china cup. The jolly station master would charge you tuppence ha'penny for a round trip to anywhere in the country and whistling porters would carry your luggage. The train would leave the station with a cheery toot and the tracks would be lined with rosy-cheeked children in pinafores and straw bonnets waving you on your way. Lovely.

Where's it all gone, eh? Awful is what it is these days. If I wanted my face crammed into someone's sweaty armpit while getting kicked in the shins and sworn at I'd go round to the wife's sister's, wouldn't I? At least I wouldn't have to spend all afternoon looking at a picture of a John Thomas some yobbo's scratched on the window or take out a second mortgage to get through the door.

They used to be the pride of Britain, the railways. We bloody invented them, too. Now even the French have better trains than us. The bloody French! And they can make them run on time, too. You don't get any of this leaves on the line, wrong type of snow, passenger taken ill nonsense. Not that they have the decency to tell you *why* the train's late any more. Now it's some automated bint going 'We regret to announce that the train you've been standing in the rain waiting for is approximately seventeen centuries late. This is due to us all being incompetents who could not get our feet wet in a paddling pool. Still we've got your money now, so up yours.'

And the state of the bloody stations. Do not get me started. Metal seats designed to give you piles if you so much as look at them, Burger King, Burger King, Burger King, and an overpriced coffee shop selling fancy styrofoam. What's wrong with a cup with a handle instead of serving the tasteless dishwater at the temperature of Vesuvius in a paper cup? It's sadism, that's what it is. These bastards like to watch you juggling it from one hand to the other and trying to suck some life back into your fingers while you negotiate your way around Knickerbox. You'll drop it in the end, of course, everyone does. And then where will you be? Hopping around the thong section with third-degree burns, the front of your trousers steaming and the staff calling the transport police, that's where.

Bloody railways.

The London Underground

It's deep underground, populated by the living dead, hot and sweaty, smells sulphurous and is constant agony from start to finish. Remind you of anywhere? That's right, when Dante wrote *The Inferno* and described the *circles* of Hell he missed one out, didn't he? The fact that the tube's got a 'Circle Line' is a dead giveaway in my opinion. Yes, when they built the London Underground there were dark forces at work.

As you enter the portal to the Underground the gloomy décor, the dirt and the smell will start taking the bloom off your mood, but this is just the beginning. Now you've got to pay, which means either dealing with surly staff or a surly machine. Either way you're looking at a significant rise in blood pressure and the loss of a sizable sum. After that it's not too bad for a while. A few people will be flapping their Oyster cards about to no avail it's true, causing a small scrum for the ticket barrier, but after that there's a pleasant ride down the escalator to look forward to, accompanied by some maestro of the tom-toms. If you looked over though, you'd see the passengers opposite struggling to climb the out-of-order up escalator. A portent of things to come.

Wait until you get down to the platform. Rats, mice, armpits, peeling adverts for holiday destinations that make you all too aware of the hellhole you're currently standing in, freaks who look like they'd give their right arm to push you in front of a train … they're all here, in spades. And if your journey takes in the Northern Line then be afraid. It's no coincidence that on the map the Northern Line is black. There will *always* be delays due to 'an incident at Morden', which everyone knows means some inconsiderate sod has jumped on the track. I suppose you can't really blame him. All he's got to look forward to is having his shoulder dislocated in the scrum for the door then an hour jammed into a meat wagon with a puke-encrusted vagrant banging away on a guitar he can't play even though it's only got one string, the occasional fart wafting past his nose and some pervert's 'briefcase' jabbing him in the back. It's enough to make anyone want to top themselves.

So you've finally made it onto a train after the sixth attempt. Though it's like being on the inside of one of those car crushers only with added body odour, at least you're on the move. The only trouble is you'll have to change twice, so you've got to go through the whole rigmarole again and then face a two-mile hike on the up escalator which is out of order. It's only ever the up escalators that don't work.

Eventually you'll emerge into whatever daylight London can muster that day, but you'll be a different person. Your clothes smell, your skin has a light patina of grease and your soul is tarnished by fear, rage and a unique condition I can only describe as tube-aaaarghh-culosis.

Cyclists

It's not the actual cycling I object to. It's a free country and if you want legs like two sticks of wilted celery then that's your right as a citizen. Just so long as cyclists keep off the roads when there's motorists about, then I say good luck to them and I hope they enjoy sucking up my fumes while they get to their optimal heart rate. No, as far as I'm concerned cyclists are welcome to share the pavement with pedestrians. What does get right up my nose though is the bloody Lycra. What happened? Did Parliament pass a bit of legislation that says cyclists aren't allowed to wear a decent pair of shorts with a bit of room in them? It's a disgrace. Wrinkly old beggars twice my age leaning over the handlebars and wafting their sweaty backsides in the air wearing nothing but a pair of shorts so tight you can see what they had for breakfast. Filthy.

While I'm on the subject, a word of advice: if you ever meet a cyclist who has momentarily dismounted, do not on any account allow your gaze to take in anything south of the waist. What you see there may put you off a boiled potato and sausage supper for life. Now, I'm a broadminded chap and what you do in the privacy of your own home is up to you. If that involves wrapping the old meat and two veg in clingfilm then I won't stand in your way. But for crying out loud, imagine if I draped the old feller out the window while I was driving, to flap about in the breeze like a dog's tongue. Imagine it! There would be an uproar, and quite rightly so. All I'm saying to cyclists is that if I have to practise self-restraint then I expect the same regard for public decency in return.

I've got two words for them: Cycle. Clips.

Budget Flights

As a general rule of thumb, if it's got 'budget' written on it you can count me in, except that budget food they sell in supermarkets which tastes like the scrapings out of a pig's knickers. But budget flights? Oh no, no, no. I'm naming no names, but it stands to reason that at £1.99 each way plus taxes you're not going to get the same kind of quality aircraft and engineering know-how. In fact, I would not be at all surprised if every craft in the budget fleet was a second-hand Aeroflot rust bucket, crawling with metal fatigue and its wings held on with sticky-backed plastic. In my humble opinion, when it comes to flying if you pay peanuts, you get dropped out of the sky from four miles up in a hail of burning wreckage. Now, when I get on a plane I want a team of highly trained engineers inspecting every inch of it with magnifying glasses before, during and after the flight. I'm funny like that. I want a bag with a tiny tube of toothpaste in and I want a pilot whose voice has broken. Little touches that are worth paying a few quid extra for. Talking of which, it may cost pennies each way on the interweb, but once you've paid the taxes and two hundred times the cost of your ticket to take a suitcase on *and* bought a cup of tea, you could have got a chauffeur-driven limo to drive you there.

And anyway, budget flights take all the romance out of flying. In my day getting on a plane was a once-in-a-lifetime experience. You scrubbed up special, wore your Sunday best and were whizzed in style to some glamorous destination like Torremolinos with a home-cooked hot meal on the way. If you asked nicely one of the cabin crew would give you a quick knee-trembler in the lavatory. Nowadays, you're jammed into a seat a battery hen would turn its beak up at, next to a bunch of shell-suited riff-raff who shouldn't have been allowed out of borstal let alone the country and end up at a shed in someone's back garden in the arse-end of the former Soviet Union. On board, the in-flight entertainment consists of trying to guess how many layers of make-up the Essex-born stewardess is wearing and checking out the window to make sure the engines are still attached. You have to buy your own peanuts at fifty quid a pop and the drinks come in little plastic cups. Little. Plastic. Cups. Says it all really.

THE
WORKING
WEEK

Open-plan Offices

An office, as nature intended, is a nice little room with one desk, one chair, one occupant. In such a place, a chap can lean back with a cup of tea and a macaroon to enjoy the newspaper without his boss glaring from across the room. He can concentrate on the crossword without people gabbling about work all over the place. He can phone the bookie to place a five-pound each-way bet on Charlie's Biscuit in the 3.15 without anyone being the wiser. Take these simple things away and what are you left with? A drone. An automaton, without dignity or hope.

They'll tell you it's a fiscally imperative space-saving measure, or that it's good for team morale. These are lies. Open-plan offices exist for one reason and one reason only. To make the smug git who does still have an office to himself feel like Lord God Almighty.

He'll use any excuse to call you at your desk. Not bother to get off his arse and come and see you, mind, but call you on the telephone at your desk in the open-plan office to say, 'Would you mind stepping in for a moment?' You'll go, feeling like a naughty schoolboy, to find the smarmy toad swivelling gently in his leather chair surrounded by neat little personal touches. All friendliness, he'll ask you to take a seat in the rickety old chair on the side of the desk in the office that has been feng-shuied especially to make you feel like a heretic before the Grand Inquisitor. Then he'll ask you some silly question that he doesn't really want an answer to, for the whole point of the exercise has been to remind you, once again, that he has an office and you don't.

Open-plan offices undermine basic human rights. Plus you can guarantee the same bloody cold is going to go round and round and round and round …

What Happened to Secretaries?

Ah, those were the days. When men were men and every young girl in the country wanted to be a secretary when she grew up. There was none of this 'women in the boardroom' nonsense. Or anywhere but click-clacking away behind their typewriters. Our glass ceiling was more of a glass carpet really and we were happy like that. The little be-stockinged lovelies were content to answer your calls, bring you a cup of tea just the way you liked it every half-hour and generally treat you like a Caliph. They came in all sorts of flavours too: from the sexily stern and efficient to the cheeky lap-sitters and all the way back to stern and efficient again. Plus there was a built-in obsolescence. Once they got to a certain age, they'd want to go off and get married and start a family. The husband would be taking care of them from now on so she wouldn't be coming back all matronly, demanding time off to pop babies out and generally waving varicose veins at you. No, after a quick whip-round for the silver-plated fish slice and a lip-trembling farewell you could take delivery of a younger, fresher model and start all over again. No severance pay, no industrial tribunal. Of course some poor sod would occasionally get stuck with a trout-faced spinster, but you could always fast-track her to Head of Switchboard.

Fast-forward thirty years and where have they all gone? An entire breed of spunky British girls vanished into thin air. The Golden Age has passed and these days you couldn't find a pert dolly bird with a pencil through her bun if your life depended on it. At the top – and only the very very top – you might get a Personal Assistant, but they're almost worse. A reminder of what you might have had in the good old days, but with none of the charm. You'll be lucky to get some harassed mother-of-four who's always on the school run or falling asleep at her desk and who'll expect *you* to make a cup of tea for *her*. Or even worse than that, a man. A bloke secretary, if you can imagine such a thing. A great hairy ape sitting on your knee and sucking saucily on the end of his pen. Well, no thank you very bloody much.

A pox on dungaree-wearing, spiky-haired feminists and so-called civil rights lawyers. Bring back the secretaries.

The Office Kitchen

You don't have to be crazy to work here, but it helps. There's always one, isn't there? The one with their own mug, which has the potential to start a fist-fight if touched without permission. All glassy eyes and fixed grin, they'll ask politely if you wouldn't mind using one of the other mugs, all the while giving the distinct impression that if you're caught mug-napping again they'll have a psychotic episode and beat you to death with it. Once they've retrieved it they'll scuttle off back to the kitchen clutching their precious 'comedy' mug like Gollum and conspicuously bleach it as if bubonic plague victims had been squeezing their boils into it.

It's usually the same person that arbitrarily appoints themselves kitchen monitor. Ruler of their own tiny domain and go-to person when the milk's run out. Whenever you pop in to make a round of teas you'll find them wiping down the surfaces and putting things away; grumbling, grumbling, always soddin' grumbling about 'the state that people leave the kitchen in' then sending around emails saying, 'Could we all pleeeeeeease make an effort to clear up the crumbs after making toast.' The thing is that even though the cleaners come in every day and no one asked them to do it, they'll still get upset because they never get thanked for taking the trouble. And I'll tell you why. It's because everyone knows that this is the classic work-avoidance technique of the office Nazi. Rather than sit in their cubicle and get on with what they're paid to do, they'll stand in the kitchen moaning at people, wiping up sticky coffee rings with an air of martyrdom, dishing out withering glances if someone leaves a buttery knife in the sink and pointedly putting clean teaspoons in the sugar pot. If someone is stupid enough to call them on it they'll look horrified that they could possibly be accused of being workshy when they spend literally *hours* a day disinfecting the kettle and tidying the fridge. Cue monumental tantrum and an email saying, 'From now on everyone can clean up their own bloody mess.' But they won't be able to help themselves. It's a compulsion. Two days later, there they'll be scrubbing away at a microscopic speck of Marmite and sighing heavily whenever anyone comes in.

Human Resources Departments

I loathe Human Resources with a venom formerly reserved for Piers Morgan. They produce nothing except migraines for anyone that comes in contact with them and they've got exactly nothing to do, which means Human Resources make stuff up to justify their existence. In practice this means meddling, paperwork, 'procedures' and employee handbooks, 'enabling personnel' and basically getting on everyone's nipples.

An example. All companies occasionally employ some workophobic sociopath by mistake. They're difficult to spot. Often the workophobic sociopath is smart, intelligent and enthusiastic in interviews. He or she will come armed with a glowing reference just because their present employer is tap-dancing around the place at the thought of seeing the back of them. However, once the three-months probation period is up they'll quickly reveal their true character: lounging around emailing their chums and playing solitaire will become second nature to them; they'll have more sick days than the average corpse, and be less productive when they do deign to come into the office; they will assassinate your character like a Borgia because you took the liberty of asking for April's sales figures. There's only one course of action and that's to get shot of the workophobic sociopath *tout suite*. Now, it used to be that a manager could take a member of staff aside and have a more or less quiet word, giving them ten minutes to clear their desk after which they'd be on their way to the dole office with a flea in their ear and a wobbling bottom lip. That's right and proper. But get Human Resources on the case and you've got a disaster on your hands. Just sack someone? Perish the thought. They'll tell you that there are all sorts of guidelines, policies and procedures to follow; verbal warnings, written warnings, arbitration meetings, key performance indicators to be put in place and additional training to be given. And of course *they* won't be doing any of it, they'll just give you another sheaf of paper and tell you to get on with it. Besides, they'll say, just sacking people is antithetical to the company's employee pledge as set out in the handbook and also we've just joined an Investing in Arseholes scheme. What will *they* say if they hear we go about sacking people?

The end result: showing the door to some turd who knows his employment rights inside out and thinks of BDSM gear as acceptable office attire is slightly more difficult to organise than a Middle East peace conference. You'll spend a year arguing with HR and in the meantime the rest of the staff will wonder why they bother doing any work either, your department will go to pot and you'll be handed your P45 by the boss with HR mugging away in the background.

Obviously, you cannot sack HR departments. My advice is garlic, holy water and a pointed stick.

Meetings Culture

Staff meetings, finance meetings, brainstorm meetings, scheduling meetings, infrastructure meetings, client meetings, I'm sorry he's in a meeting and the post boy's feeling left out because no one invited him to a meeting meeting ... the world's gone meeting crazy. You can't get into the building these days without tripping over a smokers' rights meeting, then it's the daily progress and report meeting and after that you're off, into the day's work, which comprises meeting after meeting after soddin' meeting until it gets to the point where you can only communicate with the aid of a flip pad and overhead projector. No word of a lie, I've come home on more than one occasion, written the word 'DINNER' on the kitchen tiles in blue magic marker, underlined it three times, then tried to brainstorm what to have for tea with the wife. And what do they achieve, these meetings? Enough hot air to heat a small town and not even a plate of Jaffa Cakes on the table these days.

I'm no anthropologist, but from close observation I would suggest that a small evolutionary step has occurred in the human race and hitherto gone unnoticed. *Homo sapiens* have adapted to meetings.

You see it every day. As soon as the door closes and everyone takes their seat, every face around the table goes slack as each meetingee enters what I call 'meeting space'. In meeting space, each person slips into a virtually comatose state with brain activity reduced to almost nothing. Fleeting thoughts such as what the person sitting opposite them would look like naked may be experienced, or residual brain patterns might prompt aimless doodling on Post-it Notes. To all intents and purposes the brain becomes non-functioning, though – crucially – a tiny, tiny portion of the consciousness remains alert for visual and audible clues, such as the sound of their name or someone pointing at them, which will immediately provoke the meetingee to talk at length, espousing views, giving opinions and offering statistics, again without appearing to engage the brain in any significant way. Of course, while in this vegetative state the first thing that everyone suggests is another meeting. And so they multiply, trapping us all in an endless web.

Conferences and Industry Fairs

Take your average drill-bit salesman. Three hundred and sixty-four days of the year he's earnestly selling drill bits and coming home to the wife every night, tired but content after a hard day's toil. And then Drill Bit Expo. All the latest advances in drill-bit technology under one roof and he's got an expenses-paid weekend in a four-star hotel and conference centre in Skegness. Drill-bit manufacturers hoping to secure his loyalty have flooded the hotel with models whose job it is to sit on a huge revolving drill bit wearing hot pants and a boob tube.

All he has to do is remain sober and professional, but

the madness takes hold before he's even checked in. There are drill-bit co-workers he hasn't seen since last year littering the reception area, as well as that young Mandy who's already shaping up to be one of the best drill-bit salespeople in the West Yorkshire area and it would be rude not to have a pint, wouldn't it?

Three hours later he's laying on the bar with his trousers round his ankles and someone pouring tequila into his mouth. Young Mandy's got her drill bits out and is flashing them round the room.

Six hours later he's staggering out of the lift as well as he can with young Mandy's tongue down his throat and her hand down the front of his briefs. Finally they get to his room where he orders a bottle of champagne and settles down for three hours of drunken pawing in front of a pay-per-view adult movie.

Twelve hours later young Mandy's crawling around on the floor searching for her knickers and looking like the Bride of Frankenstein while he tries desperately to make his face appear normal and ignore the credit-card receipt that is telling him that yes, he did spend the company's annual profit in the bar last night. The hangover is threatening to push the actual eyeballs out of his head, and the wife chooses that moment to phone and find out how it's going.

Then there's twelve sales meetings on the trot, in a Suits You suit that's still got traces of sick on it, a quick shower and off to the bar to start all over again.

We've all been there. The disciplinary action when the hotel bill hits accounts and the bottle of the champagne you put on the room tab and only drank half of turns out to have been £3,000-a-bottle Dom Perignon and the divorce proceedings when Mandy's knickers finally turn up in the suitcase. Conferences and Industry Fairs are little more than business-sponsored debauchathons and shag-fests. They wreck lives and they wreck marriages. They should be banned.

IT Departments

Every office has them these days. A little nest of jumped-up geeks and wonks who make incomprehensible jokes about database programming, spend the day furtively playing *Civilisation IV* behind a screen of semi-dismantled computers and always, always let their phone go to voicemail, because 'We're upgrading the server at the moment', which – by the way – translates as 'We're looking at pictures of Heidi Klum at the moment'. The leader – he'll call himself the IT Director – will be as arrogant as King Wolfgang the Condescending, make you grovel for two days before dealing with the slightest problem and earn twice as much as you. His troop of sixteen-year-old lackeys will wear Nine Inch Nails T-shirts to work and maintain an air of superiority despite the fact that they've never spoken to a girl. Even though you've been with for the company for twenty years and they do nothing but play with themselves in front of their computers when they think no one's looking, even the most junior member of the IT staff will be on a package you can only dream of.

You might be getting the impression that I'm just the tiniest bit fed up with the IT boys, but I'm not the sort of nerdist who goes around hating people just because they know what USB stands for. No, what gets my goat is the big IT secret.

As a whole, the IT department have not the faintest clue what it is the company actually does – all they know is that they have you utterly, totally at their mercy. And why? Because all business is now conducted by email and they, and only they, have the arcane knowledge that keeps the email working. If email goes down everyone would have to actually pick up the phone to the person they've been dealing with for eight years, but have only ever communicated by email. They'd have to write *letters*. Do *filing*. Go and *see people*. It would all be too unspeakably horrid for words and cannot be allowed to happen. And so the IT Department has them by the short and curlies. But the time of liberation is near. After long years of espionage I have discovered the secret that keeps the email working. The secret that means the end of the IT Department holding us all hostage. It's a number. A simple number that they keep hidden like a priceless treasure, for it is the key to their fortune. In reality the IT Department have no knowledge whatsoever of how to fix email. What they do have is the telephone number to the *free* Outlook Express helpline …

Synergy and Other Business Speak

FYI, a heads-up: talking twaddle and gibberish is totally excremental. Like your stupid gelled-back hair it doesn't make you look like a plugged-in international player, it makes you look like a complete moron.

What happened here? When did the Queen's English become open to abuse from Chardonnay-drinking greasy-pole climbers? I'm sitting in meetings these days and it's a nonstop deluge of buzzwords and jargon. Irritating? It's like someone's rubbing a cheese grater across your brain. Marketing have got their 'ducks in a row', which is apparently a 'no-brainer', sales are 'leveraging a deliverable ETA' and I've been asked to go off and 'facilitate synergy building'. We're all going to 'connect ear-to-ear' on Friday for the purposes of 'reviewage', but we mustn't think of it as a 'blamestorm', because 'hey, we don't *do* blame culture'.

What? No-speako-the-lingo. I haven't got the faintest idea what the buggers are on about. Admit that though and you might as well get your coat. These days the actual ability to do your job is much less important than being able to spout a never-ending stream of drivel. It got to the point where if I heard one more yuppie middle manager tell me that I have to blue sky a massive-aggressive paradigm shift, I was going to kick him in the low-hanging fruit. Then I had a revelation …

The truth is no one understands business-speak. It's like opera: no one's got a clue what's going on but you have to pretend you do or you look like a ninny. So, my advice is make up your own. So long as you use the word 'brand' every so often no one will notice the difference. When asked how the synergy's coming along, just say something like, 'We have an exemplary wardrobe facility in the synergy zone. There's still the matrix agenda of course, but it's epoch-bending so we're going to plunge the toilet on that one. And as our SPANK analysis results show, we're all about tectonic shiftage and vacuum branding. Pulling the udders, I'd say it looks like being a turd run all the way to the latrine pit.'

Look around the boardroom table and you'll see a dozen gelled heads nodding sagely and the boss will suddenly want to take you out for golf.

Working from Home

Hello, you might think, here's a chance for larks. After kissing his arse ceaselessly for years, the boss has finally let me work from home. Compared to the office, it's going to be a little slice of paradise. A haven of peaceful repose. You've got the day's itinerary all worked out: a nice lie-in followed by a leisurely breakfast in bed, watch Lorraine Kelly on the telly for a bit and check emails about ten, ten-thirty. Call into the office to remind them who you are and then lunch and a nice siesta. Maybe the missus would like to join you for a little afternoon hanky-panky while those poor beggars in the office are munching on a sandwich at their desks. Oh yes, from afar working from home looks like beer and skittles all the way. Except it's not.

Imagine an alternative scenario. You'll be wide awake by six in the morning because your body's now hard-wired to the damn alarm clock, the wife's grumpy because you're rattling around the house while she's used to some peace and quiet and if you've got kids you'll be expected to help dress and feed the also grumpy little beggars and do the school run for a change and 'No we won't be watching Lorraine Kelly, I *always* watch Jeremy Kyle in the morning.' By this time the boss is on the phone. It's only seven-thirty, but what you hadn't realised is that the vindictive bastard will be on your case every second of the day to make sure you're not skiving off, making it impossible to look at the little bit of work you did actually bring home with you. The wife will laugh in your face if you suggest hanky-panky. Instead, wherever you sit or tread there will be a hoover attacking your feet like a hungry predator. Again, if you have kids they'll be home just as you're starting to warm up to the day and shrieking around the house like escapees from a splatter movie.

And there are throngs, never-ending hordes beating a path to your front door throughout the day. The postman, the gas man, people selling double glazing, gypsies wanting to tarmac the two-inch-square front lawn. Don't these people have jobs to go to? They are as nothing against the Jehovah's Witnesses though. Now, it takes years of experience to effectively deal with the Jehovah's Witnesses and your office-based life will have left you woefully unprepared. Of course, the gleeful old lady and her younger chaperone will sense you're a Jehovah's Witness virgin just because you haven't slammed the door in their face with a firm 'piss off' and they'll play you like a violin, loving every embarrassed minute of it. Before you know it they'll be wedged into the sofa, sucking your tea down them and grinning from ear to ear while you try and squirm your way through an explanation of why you don't love Jesus quite as much as they might prefer.

Even if your office is in downtown Baghdad you're better off staying put.

Meeting and Greeting

The cheek. The bloody barefaced nerve of it. The CEO has decided that what the company really needs is a 'meet and greet' with its customers, suppliers, accountants or some such jolly band of leeches. There will be excited circular emails about the 'getting to know you session', or 'opportunity to bond face to face with our most valued clients'. Leaving aside that what he actually means is 'an opportunity to get the tight buggers pissed and screw more orders out of them', you are told to attend. Not asked; told. Well, what a great idea Mr CEO, but you'll notice the clock quite blatantly says five-thirty and anything after that is my free time, with the emphasis on the word 'free' in regards to the fact that you don't actually pay me after that point in the day, so I think I'll be getting along home now if you don't mind, thankyouverymuch.

After he's shown you what a P45 looks like, you'll be standing next to a dustbin full of the cheapest champagne you can get his hands on, trussed up in your best suit and waiting for the valued clients to arrive. Your compensation for missing out on a night in the boozer consists of little sausages on sticks and the champagne-a-like, so you'll help yourself, despite the boss's disapproving glares, thinking that some sausage might soak up the drink that will be an absolute necessity to get through this arse of an evening. Then they'll come, in little dribs and drabs, like strange scuttling creatures that crawl from under rocks. People that you have dealt with every day for years, but have never seen in the flesh. They're vastly more ugly than you could possibly have imagined and just as awkward as you at being in this strange social-gathering-in-an-office setting. You'd like to think it was awkwardness, because it's that or else they have the personalities of sandpaper.

Although you're under orders to schmooze, your every conversational sally will dry up and the only thing you can think to do is keep refreshing glasses, yours first, until you go from gawky and tongue-tied to staggeringly drunk in the space of about fifteen minutes and start regaling the 'valued clients' with stories of an intimate and wildly inappropriate nature. But for once that's OK. Awkwardness makes strange bedfellows and even the boss has been throwing it back with abandon and now has his arm round your shoulder and is telling your biggest client that he's the world's biggest tosser.

And the insane thing is that it works. The next day the orders will come pouring in – possibly in an bid to keep quiet the incident with the photocopier at two in the morning – and your smug boss will already be typing out another circular email telling you that the night was such a success he's going to make it a weekly event.

POPULAR CULTURE

'Celebrities'

'You want fame? Well fame costs, and right here's where you start paying – in sweat!' Remember those days? When young men and women in legwarmers and headbands would sweat and strain to hone their craft. Be it acting, singing or making music they were bursting with so much talent they'd quite often have to 'do the show right here in the cafeteria'.

Bet they wish they hadn't bothered now.

Nowadays all some deeply offensive troll with not enough grey matter to float a matchstick and the morals of a sex-starved badger needs to do to achieve 'celebrity' status is lounge around in bed on *Big Brother* for ten weeks, occasionally slithering out from under the duvet to swear at or screw someone. That or shag a footballer. Either way, hey presto; they've suddenly gone bright orange and have their own TV show, a weekly spot in *Hello!* magazine, book deals, sponsorships, singles coming out of their bums and their own perfume.

How did it happen? That's what I want to know. Did all the acting schools close down? Did some killer virus wipe out all the musicians? Did all the beautiful, polite, intelligent and talented people bugger off somewhere? Presumably the media folks scour the country for someone, anyone, with a breath of charisma or talent in their body and draw a total blank before they reluctantly pick up the phone to Jade bloody Goody:

'It's no good, Tarquin, I've tried the Krankies and that green bird in the nappy. Eddie the Eagle's booked up and Chegwin's people won't even get back to us. We've scraped the barrel and come up with nothing.'

'What's underneath the barrel, Sebastian?'

'Some woodlice and Jade Goody.'

'Are the woodlice available?'

'Panto in Milton Keynes.'

'Oh God Lord! We'll have to use Goody then.'

And how come everyone's suddenly lapping it up? 'Oh Jade, she's such an inspiration.' Well, yes I suppose so – if you aspire to an IQ in single digits.

It's jaw-dropping. Jodie Marsh, the *Celebrity Big Brother* contestant and former 'glamour' model, actually had a TV show where men competed to *marry* her – *Totally Jodie Marsh: Who'll take her up the aisle?* Leaving aside the fact that any man in his right mind would crawl across broken glass and hot coals *not* to marry Jodie Marsh, what sort of celebrity would do that? What are you famous for then, Jodi? Well, getting my thru'pennies out and selling my body and soul for an hour a week on a cable TV channel. How lovely, your old mam and dad must be so proud.

What really gets me though is they're all writing bloody autobiographies. And they're bestsellers! Who in God's name wants to read the life story of a 22-year-old, eh? And a 22-year-old with all the charm of a wet fart at that. Not that they write the bloody things. I tell you what, bung me fifty grand and I'll write it for you: 'Got born, was an annoyingly precocious/ill-mannered/thick (*delete as appropriate*) child. Haven't grown out of it yet.' There you go, love, now please sod off and stop polluting the environment with your pouting and whiny, self-satisfied mewling.

Not that we should worry about her for too long, of course, she'll be forgotten in three months and some other 'celeb' will take her place – oh look, here comes Peaches Geldof!

The 'cult of celebrity' they call it. Well they all look like complete cults to me.

I'm a Celebrity ...

And what do they do, these so-called celebrities? Well it appears that the height of their skill, the very zenith of their abilities, is to go and sit in the jungle once a year and moan alongside a bunch of no-hopers whose career went pear-shaped circa 1977. Of course you never get *real* celebrities on there so the show should really be called 'I'm a Has-been, Please Pay Attention to Me'. Pathetic really. The list of contestants will always include the following categories:

1 Wannabe. No real career beyond *Hello!*, the occasional Iceland commercial and reality TV shows. Nothing of interest to say. Will try and deflect attention from how dull they are by having a 'breakdown' at the earliest opportunity and/or bitching about everyone.

2   Has-been. Was drunk and/or needed the money when asked to do the show. Can't really work out why they're there and regret it almost immediately. Moan constantly and blow whatever remnants of credibility they might have had.

3   Not-really-a-celebrity-at-all. Are connected to a proper celebrity or have been in the papers once or twice. The not-really-a-celebrity-at-all contestant will be out to show how plucky and game they are in order to further their media career, but will also moan constantly when they think the camera's not on them.

4   Has-been #2. Used to be famous eons ago and would really like to be again. Like the not-really-a-celebrity-at-all contestant, their tactic will be pluck and enthusiasm, but they will also irritatingly ingratiate themselves to avoid being evicted.

5   Has-been wild card. This contestant will be genuinely certifiable and will also have some kind of breakdown.

Frankly I don't see the point in it myself. If they can't afford to get proper celebrities whose constant griping and whinging we might actually be interested in then Ant and Dec should either stop hogging airtime or have a telephone vote and find some 'celebrities' we really dislike, then alter the daily challenges a little bit. Really make the blighters work for their bush tucker. I'd be picking up the phone in a shot if I thought there was a chance to see Jade Goody wrestling a great white shark armed only with a Curly Wurly, Darren Day staked out on a nest of fire ants or Tara Palmer-Tomkinson dodging poisoned darts from blowpipes.

Talent Shows

We all love a freakshow in Britain of course. Always have. These days though it's not enough to just have the bearded ladies and world's fattest men or go on a tour round the local mental asylum like you could in the past. We're too PC for that. Instead they try and pretend it's not a freakshow at all, which is why every channel is crawling with programmes like Women Living With Facial Hair, America's Fattest, or The Truth About Tourette's. or something equally vulgar. When push comes to shove though it's all about jeering at the freaks. And best of all are the talent shows. You know the ones I mean. The ones where you can barely see the TV you're so blinded by Simon Cowell's teeth.

It is boggling the humiliation that people will put themselves through for the chance to get their ugly mug on the telly. They must practise in front of a mirror, right? They must listen to themselves sing a bit before they brave the judges' panel. They must know, deep down, that they've got a face like a monkey's scrotum and the voice of a cement mixer. Or that they're a middle-aged loony whose only resemblance to Elvis is around the waistband. They *must* have just the tiniest bit of an inkling that even the otherwise lovely Sharon Osbourne is likely to stagger off set widdling in her knickers at the sight of them.

So why? Why would you compound your already fairly miserable existence by going up in front of ten million people and making a complete and utter goon of yourself? And as if the actual performance wasn't desperate enough, why have the bloody gall to start arguing when the judges tell you you're rubbish? And have tantrums? Every episode – every one – there's some desperately unlucky adolescent who was clearly last in the line when looks, talent and charisma were being handed out flouncing down the corridor screaming, 'I'll show you, Simon. I'm going to be a star!'

So far, great TV. I'm loving it. What bothers me is not that they parade these sad, deluded fruitcakes in front of us in the name of entertainment. No, what gets me is that they have to have all the rubbish after it, where contestants with just enough talent to make them technically OK, if totally bland, mug their way through the same old Abba hits year in year out. In my book if the irresistible pull of celebrity is good for one thing it's the tempting of hopeless sad sacks from under their rocks to be pointed and laughed at. If I had my way the whole season would be called Simon Cowell's Freak Hour.

Spooks and Psychics

'Is Tomfoolery Hall really haunted? We have twenty-four hours to pull the wool over your eyes.'

Nothing is more likely to give me a loss-of-consciousness experience than the sight of full-grown people screaming the place down because they caught an 'orb' on camera. (And – by the way – that's not an 'orb'. That, my friend, is what we in the trade call 'dust'.) But every time you switch the bloody TV on these days there's psychic detectives and ghost whisperers and haunting investigators leering out at you on night-vision camera, for all the world as if ghosts really existed. Oh, they've got all the latest graphics and spooky music and effects, but what they haven't got is any ghosts. And I'll tell you why, shall I? Let you into a little secret? It's because there's no such thing as ghosts. And there were no such things as 'spiritualist mediums' either until the mid-nineteenth century. The whole movement is based on the work of three sisters, by the name of Fox, who wowed the world with their amazing table-rapping demonstrations. But guess what? That's right, they all three later confessed to being hoaxers. Charlatans. Frauds. Setting a trend you might say. And so the world should have sighed at its gullibility and gone back to not believing in ghosts. But oh no, a century later there's 'spiritualist medium' Derek Acorah – with his white thong always visible in night-vision – and his ghostly sidekick 'Sam' still rapping away at the table and going, 'What's that Sam? Mary … loves … Dick. Mary loves Dick. Thank you Sam. Mary loves Dick.' Now I don't doubt that there are people out there who hear voices in their heads, but there's a word for those people and it's *not* 'medium'. The most pitiful thing though is that there's millions out there believing *every bloody word*. They even have ardent fans sending in texts during live shows corroborating the spookiness: 'When my cat saw Derek channelling that evil spirit it pissed itself.' Well, there's nothing spooky about that mate. So did I.

There have been God knows how many series, endless hours of footage, locked-off cameras, trigger objects, and a horde of so-called psychics trampling around every stately home in the country. They've recorded squeaks, bangs, odd smells, and moths galore, but have any one of these shows produced a single shred of incontrovertible evidence? Of course not. Because there's no. Such. Thing. As. Ghosts. There's creative editing and hysterical presenters and fraudulent ex-footballers, but there's no. Such. Thing. As. Ghosts. Any old house in the country is going to make squeaks, bangs and odd smells all the time. I get the lot in my very own bedroom at night, especially if the wife's been eating pickled onions. But it's not ghosts. Because they don't exist. So stop treating us like bloody idiots and put something decent on.

Daytime 'Advice' Shows

If there's one thing guaranteed to get my blood boiling it's watching the television during the day. And especially Trisha and that Jeremy soddin' Kyle. I've read a lot of twaddle about these shows in the papers. How it's cruel to parade these poor unfortunates in front of a television audience for sport. Rubbish. I'll tell you what's cruel. Popping out kid after kid by different fathers for the benefit money. That's cruel. In my opinion these wishy-washy do-gooder TV presenters do not go anywhere near far enough. 'Oooo Jeremy,' their gurning so-called guests bleat. 'I've just had me fourteenth kid but I was so pissed on the White Lightning I can't remember who the dad was. Be a good chap and break out the DNA test would you?' Then out troop jobless monkey with bad teeth, jobless monkey with bad hair and jobless monkey with bad teeth, bad hair and sticking-out ears. Jeremy or Trisha obliges with the test, gives them a stern talking-to and off mum and dad trot to the benefit office once again.

No.

I tell you what Jeremy wants to do. And Trisha also. Once the DNA results are in, they want to get those big bald blokes they have hanging around the stage to hold down the dirty beggar, whip his pants down and perform a live-on-stage castration. It needn't be a professional job, just so long as Jeremy or Trisha can hold up his goolies afterwards for the audience at home to see. Similarly for these drunken wife-beaters they have on. Don't bother with the touchy-feely namby-pamby counselling Trisha, just put the bloody boot in. There's one of him against you and two tough-looking bouncers. You're a fit-looking lass, get some steel toecaps on and give him a taste of his own medicine. Drug addiction? Try injecting your filthy cannabis with ten broken fingers, mate. Don't like what your mam said about our Tina? Oh dear, oh dear. I tell you what love. Here's a cricket bat for your mam and a sock with a half-brick in for Tina, now they can sort it out between themselves and entertain the nation at the same time.

Now that would be morning TV worth getting up for.

Oasis

Imagine the sound of an industrial abattoir with a retarded donkey repeatedly braying the word 'Sonsheeyine'. There you have Oasis. This bunch of foul-mouthed layabouts consist of a Beatles impersonator, a badly shaved gibbon, Ringo Starr's son and a couple of other blokes no one takes any notice of. They are famous for inventing 'Britpap' in the 1990s and used to hang out with Tony Blair. Also known for fighting amongst themselves on stage, it is alleged (by me) that their aggressive attitude and wild lifestyles encouraged the former prime minister to invade Iraq. Quite simply, I reckon Blair wanted to look 'a bit tasty' in front of his new friends. Oasis are thus the first band in UK history to have started a war.

In my opinion, every member of Oasis would benefit from a birching and a stint in the army. Failing that, a haircut and a makeover with Lorraine Kelly. They are not a patch on Herman's Hermits or Wayne Fontana and the Mindbenders, though I suppose you can't put all the blame at their feet. The musical rot set in for Manchester with that pasty-faced, ginger pillock from Simply Red. Still, you'd have thought after him the city council would have taken steps to prevent its citizens inflicting this kind of noise pollution on the rest of us.

Apparently Oasis go down well at the Hoodie's Arms, but they are not my cup of tea at all.

Drug Addict Pop Stars

In the old days we had proper pop stars like Cliff Richard and the Beverley Sisters. Decent people with respectful haircuts who could hold a note and would scrub up smart for *Saturday Night at the Palladium*. And then the sixties arrived and suddenly they're all at it. Smoking LCD, jacking up pot into their eyeballs, sniffing weeds. The music suffered of course, which is why Sir Cliff was still knocking out classics like 'Wired for Sound' long after all the Beatles could manage was weird druggie nonsense like *Sergeant Pepper's Lonely Hearts Club Band*. Since the sixties it's never been the same. Oh, there have been a few brave pop stars who 'just say no', like the Osmonds and Steps – and doesn't the quality shine through, eh? – but mostly the record industry is now full of dirty long-hairs floating round the place in their loon pants and beads. They think it gives them some kind of glamour, like they're a proper tortured artist not just some jumped-up crooner or guitar player, but what's so glamorous about choking to death on your own puke? Or having a heart attack on the loo?

And it never ceases to amaze me that if you or I were caught sniffing ecstasy or munching down the crack tablets we'd be straight in the slammer, but just because some constipated, gurning lowlife has had a record out they can evade prison almost indefinitely. I was under the impression that possession of a class A drug was a *crime*. Which makes these people *criminals*. To my mind that means a few years inside stitching mailbags or at the very least a public flogging. But, oh no, it's all sympathy and trying to save them from themselves. All right so that Pete Doherty got banged up eventually, but only for about twenty minutes and after what, three million convictions? The bloke's virtually going into court with a rolled-up twenty-pound note hanging out his nose and doing everything but snorting heroin off the judge's bench and they've still asked him nicely to run along to rehab, which – of course – means a couple of days of intense massage therapy in a five-star hotel and then a massive drug binge to celebrate getting out. And then he'll say he's quit, but we all know that he's only stopped because he's wiped out the entire nation's supply during one party. As soon as the Afghan poppy harvest is in he's soon back to his old tricks.

That Winehouse is another one. Splashed all over the papers so stoned her eyes are pointing in different directions, cancelling concerts left, right and centre because she's sky-high in la-la land and if she does eventually manage to crawl out onto the stage she's in no fit state to give the punters their money's worth. And what happens? Not even rehab for our Amy. Oh, they'll try and make her all right, but she'll say no, no, no.

Rap Music

So that's music these days, is it? Gangsters with their bums hanging out doing odd things with their hands and banging on about popping a cap in someone's arse; young women wiggling their backsides hypnotically and talking dirty; the sound of a pneumatic drill with some halfwit shouting about bitches over the top. Bloody charming. Guaranteed to put a spring in your step and have you whistling along, that is.

'Oh, it's *authentic*,' the bleeding-heart liberals say. 'It's what life is like in the 'hood.' Well, not in my bloody 'hood it's not. If it's that bad in downtown LA they want to think about moving round my way. They can buy kristal champagne at $10,000 a bottle, so I'm sure they could afford that nice little semi that's on the market just down the road. No beggar's going to drive by with an AK47 spraying you with bullets and Mr Patel's shop on the corner does some very nice 2-for-1 deals . Give them a couple of weeks to settle in and they'll soon be rapping about mowing the lawn, washing the motor of a Sunday morning and the benefits of a quiet career in accountancy. But no, apparently we're not keeping it *real* enough down my street. *Real* life is all about offing people, dealing drugs, banging bitches, how much respect you got and having people give you loads of money for doing nothing more than shouting obscenities.

And that's why every time I go into town there's some posse of middle-class teenagers with their trousers round their knees sneering at everyone. Thank you rappers and music industry for colluding with the TV, movie and video-game people to bring up a generation of children on a steady diet of violence. What a fantastic idea that was. Twenty years ago they'd have been hanging round the door with garden tools wanting to do bob-a-job, now the only hoe they're interested in is some pregnant fourteen-year-old with her hair scraped back so hard her eyes are up round her ears. That is if they can stop stabbing and shooting each other for five minutes.

Respect? You want some respect you can wash your filthy mouth out and pull your bloody trousers up.

Digital Music

I remember watching *Tomorrow's World* back in the eighties with Judith Hann waving the first ever CDs around and raving about how great they were. She was smearing jam on them, rubbing them with sandpaper, running over them with a tank, then slipping them in the CD player and going 'ta da' when they still played clear as a bell. For a generation that was used to jogging the stuck needle every two minutes, dragging funny-smelling cleaning blocks over records and likely to murder anyone who left your latest Dave Clark Five album out of its sleeve, it was a bloody miracle. We thought we'd never need to replace a scratched record again – CDs are the future, Judith told us, CDs are forever. Yes, well I'm sure you said that about the personal jet-pack and the Sinclair C5 too, love, but perhaps you could be onto something for once, so we all rushed out and paid a small fortune to replace our old vinyl with reflective polycarbonate plastic.

My reasons for now considering legal action against Judith are twofold. Firstly CDs last hardly any time at all. Leave them laying around on the floor for six months or use them as coasters more than a few dozen times and they get knackered the same as records, only this time you can't push the needle along. Second, after less than three decades suddenly CDs are out and downloads are in and you've got to pay for your *Best of Mario Lanza* all over again *and* buy another new stereo to play it on. Only it's not a proper stereo that can sit in the corner of the room and impress the neighbours this time, it's a little bit of white plastic that looks more like a Milky Bar. It's the size of my thumbnail and keeps getting lost down the back of the sofa. You don't get a record sleeve, so you can't sing along and as far as I can tell they haven't even bothered digitising Nana Mouskouri. And the worst thing is, all those lovely vinyl records I threw in the bin are now collector's items and worth a mint.

You lied, Judith. Thanks very much.

Lads' Mags

There's no other explanation: today's chaps have the brain capacity of your average goldfish. How else would lads' mags get away with it? Anyone with even the tiniest bit of sense would take one look and say, 'Here's some pictures of ladies' breasts, here's an article about the staff getting drunk, some video-game reviews, here's a few cars, but only a few because market research say men like drinking, video games and bosoms more than cars these days, and – hello – a few more boobs. All fine and dandy, but wasn't that exactly what they put in last month?' It's true. Exactly the bleeding same each and every month and each and every magazine. What a job that must be every month. You can imagine the production meeting:

'Right, it's Bob's turn to shuffle the pictures around this month, the rest of you down to the pub.'

'But it's starting to look a bit samey, Charlie.'

'Well, swap some booby pictures with our competitors

and put that article in about Hunter S. Thompson again. The punters like Hunter S. Thompson. He was a proper lad was Hunter and though none of the readers have ever got past page two of *Fear and Loathing in Las Vegas* it gives the mag an intellectual air and make them feel we don't think they're complete idiots when we're ripping them off four quid for the same old rubbish yet again.'

'Right you are, Charlie. That'll take me a couple of hours so line up a few pints for me, then I can fail to chat up the barmaid, wee on myself, and throw up everywhere. It'll make a nice feature.'

'You did that last month.'

'All right this time, I'll wee on the barmaid, throw up everywhere and fail to chat myself up.'

'Brilliant Bob, no wonder you earn fifty grand a year.'

POLITICS

Politicians

Some bright spark, G. B. Shaw methinks, once said, 'He knows nothing; and thinks he knows everything. That points clearly to a political career.' And he was right. What a shower. Lying bunch of hopeless, mendacious, arrogant, incompetent nest-featherers who promise the earth every five years and as soon as they're in power spend every waking hour doing their best to bugger up the country and make everyone's lives as miserable as possible. Most of them can't even get a haircut right, so what hope have they got for running the country?

In my opinion politicians are unfit for purpose by dint of wanting to become politicians in the first place. These were the kids who instead of playing footie in the park formed a *debating society*, the snide little gits whose deepest desire was to be head boy or girl. When they got to university they weren't drinking pints of snakebite, wearing their pants on their head and lying around in bed all day like every other normal student, they weaselled their way into the Student Union and strutted around the place with a little flock of hangers-on, dictating to everyone and never getting laid, thus laying the founda-tions of some vile perversion. What people fail to understand is that such specimens are quite rightly shunned as children and young adults. We have an instinctive aversion to know-it-all speccy little nerds whose idea of a good time is arguing about the 1842 Corn Laws, because – and this is the clincher – we can *sense* that they're little bloody politicians in the making. This fosters a deep-seated resentment in them, which when they are elected to power by an electorate duped by a carefully crafted and entirely fictional 'normal' persona, manifests itself in nasty, spiteful policies like banning smoking in pubs and invading countries willy-nilly. QED, you see?

If we have to have a government, why not fill it up with people who'd usually run screaming from the idea of being a politician? Kick out the oik with a degree in archaeology and delusions of grandeur and drag an Economics Professor or the CEO of a successful company in to be Chancellor of the Exchequer. Force someone with a little bit of style and charisma to be Prime Minister rather than elect a compulsive liar with a personality bypass and an inability to discern arse from elbow. That Sir Ian McKellen, for example, would make a great national figurehead. How jealous would all the other countries be when they realised we had Gandalf as our PM? And every time someone tried to put through an unpopular bit of legislation, he could wave the speaker's mace around and do the 'Thou shall not pass' speech. Marvellous.

Prime Minister's Questions

If you want to get a flavour of how these chumps operate, watch *Prime Minister's Questions*. There they'll be, the country's statesmen and women, our dignified leaders to whom we look for guidance and support. Forged in the white-hot furnace of democracy, these are our elected representatives. Caretakers of this great nation. Who – incidentally – get paid by the bucketload with more perks than you could shake a stick at. And how do these blithering bloody idiots behave? Something like this:

Spineless Backbench Sycophant: Will my right honourable friend join me in agreeing that purple is his favourite colour?

Cue eruption of paper dart throwing, jeers and catcalls from the opposition.

Speaker: Order, order. If you don't settle down none of you will be going on the swings at playtime.

Prime Minister: Thank you, Mr Speaker. I'd like to begin by agreeing with the right honourable member for Wotton Downs, purple is my favourite colour, and also draw his attention to this lovely drawing of a purple boat the Home Secretary did for me yesterday.

Speaker: Leader of the opposition.

LOTO: We in the opposition also think that purple is a nice colour, but would the Prime Minister agree that he smells of poos … and wees?

Stamping of feet, screams and gibbering, pointing and laughing.

PM: Mr Speaker ... Mr Speaker. The findings of our most recent enquiry show categorically that the odour of poos and wees in this government has fallen dramatically by three per cent over the last fiscal quarter ...

Opposition benches: Wee breath! Farty pants!

Speaker: Order! If I have to tell you again it will be smacked bottoms all round ...

PM: ... And furthermore, the same enquiry has produced evidence that the right honourable leader of the opposition has fleas. He should look to his fleas before accusing us of wees!

PM sits down looking smug at his neat turn of phrase to roars and screeches from both benches.

Speaker: That's it. No story time this afternoon.

And so it will go on. A disgusting display of bad manners and foul-mouthed name-calling. As the camera pans round you'll see a number of old duffers asleep and drooling, the Foreign Secretary with her finger jammed up her nose to the third knuckle and the Liberal Democrat leader sulking because no one's paying him any attention. Again.

And they call Britain the cradle of democracy. Ha, bloody crèche of democracy is more like it.

Big Brother Society

Any day now it's coming. The CCTV camera in every toilet so that the government can get some computer program (MicrosoftGillianMcKeithV1.27) to analyse your motions and issue personalised dietary guidelines. And if you think it'll never happen, just take a look around. Every time you close the front door there's some hidden camera peering at you, some creepy government henchman watching you pick your nose or play pocket billiards or looking down ladies' blouses. A digital swarm is spreading across the country prying into everyone's lives and getting ever closer to coming inside your actual house.

They *say* it's to provide security, which is a load of old bobbins as usual. Cameras don't prevent crimes and the reason is this: even the most ill-educated street rodent knows that all he has to do is pull his hood up while he's beating the pension out of some geriatric and no one's the wiser. No, surveillance cameras aren't meant to prevent crime, they're stage one in an insidious plot to monitor and control each and every one of us. Stage two is recording every telephone call we make and reading all email we send. Apparently this is to help prevent terrorism, as if any terrorist is going to be stupid enough to write an email like this:

Re: Terrorist Suicide Bomb Plot
To: Abdullah;
CC: All Al Qaeda Staff;

Hi Abdullah,

Hope you are well, lovely weather for a picnic bomb, isn't it?

Just a quick one to say good luck with the suicide bomb on the number 345 at 10.20am on the 1st of May, just outside HMV on Oxford Street. I'd say keep up the good work, but well, you know ... Anyway TTFN, have fun out there and don't forget to wear a warm vest, ha ha.

Love
Osama B xx

No, they'll use code. Of course they'll use a soddin' code! Which means any useful anti-terrorism information will be impossible to find within the ten billion other emails sent that day. See, it's not really about terrorism, it's about a nasty, suspicious government worming its way into every tiny part of your life. Pretty soon you won't be able to have a little hanky-panky with the wife without some apparatchik telling you by remote that you're not making love in the party-permitted manner.

What paranoid claptrap, you might say, but look at the evidence. Governments don't trust the people. Schools are turning out drones who can pass government-approved tests, but wouldn't know an independent thought if it was hanging off their earring, youngsters can't have an impromptu party in a field in the middle of nowhere any more, there's politically correct legislation slowly curtailing free speech, the government are constantly banging on about what you should eat, drink and smoke, your every tiny detail is on a government database somewhere in Swindon and all the while the cameras are zooming in closer and closer. And if that lot doesn't strike you as sinister just wait for stage three: ID cards. 'Papers? Vhere are your papers?' Sound familiar?

When George Orwell wrote *1984* it was supposed to be a warning, not a bloody how-to guide.

The Law

Where do they get judges these days? It's like they rounded up all the social workers who were sacked for being too wet, stuck wigs on them and pushed them into the courts. There's one sitting behind every bench; so limp-wristed he needs splints to hold the bloody gavel and with less common sense than a *Guardian* columnist. I mean, what goes through their minds? Some poor bloke's been stabbed by 'youths' because he had the cheek to ask them politely to stop kicking him and the perpetrators eventually come in front of the beak. Now you or I would see a pack of vermin who needs sixty licks of the cat, at least ten years and what a shame they got rid of the noose. But your average *judge* sees a huddled mass of poor, disadvantaged urchins like something out of a Dickens novel, bless their little hearts. The government must have let them down terribly, but they'd flourish if only given the chance. That *bastard* they stabbed is yet another example of the oppression that faces these delicate flowers every day. So, off you go little ones, run free with the bunnies and don't forget to pick up your sharpened screwdrivers from mean old PC Plod on the way out. The only other explanation I can think of is that the judges are all suffering from Alzheimer's or are so far round the twist they think they're Simon Cowell voting for the best under-sixteens boy band. But they wouldn't let mentally deficient judges try cases, would they? Of course not.

The end result is prisons are overflowing with folk who traumatised some pond life ransacking their house by asking him to leave and pensioners slammed up for bruising some poor villain's knuckles with their face. Mind you, prison's probably the best place to be these days. They're full of decent, law-abiding citizens and all the riff-raff are on the outside over a thirty-foot wall topped with razor wire. Plus, you never know; you might get to meet Jeffrey Archer.

Still, I don't care what the law says; if you start wandering around my house in the middle of the night, stealing the food off my table and taking a crap on the carpet, I'm going to shoot you. Unless you're the dog of course, in which case I'm just going to tear my hair out, grit my teeth and *threaten* to shoot you. Again.

The Family

I'm sick and bloody tired of hearing about the days when we had a copper on every street corner fetching kids a clip round the ear where appropriate and generally keeping law and order. Urban myth. Touch of the old rose-tinteds. Oh, we had policemen all right, but they were pretty much the same as coppers these days. Spending weeks at a time in the station sucking a pencil and wondering how to spell 'proceeding'. No, they never did much apart from drink tea and weed the flowerbeds, because there was no need. In those days we had a much more effective and brutal crime deterrent. It was called 'mum'. And no, I don't mean some sixteen-year-old mother of twelve who doesn't know which way on a condom goes let alone how to raise a family, or some poor, frazzled creature who works twelve-hour days to pay for childminders and comes home to a pile of washing like Kilimanjaro; I mean a proper mum. With eyes in the back of her head, a forearm that could stop a charging rhino and the mind-reading talent of Uri Geller. You could be six miles away, hidden in undergrowth with your first ever packet of John Players or a dirty magazine you'd found in the woods and a hand would reach out of nowhere and grab you by the ear. Then you'd be dragged home with mum bawling, 'Just wait till your father hears about this,' though – of course – it wasn't your dad you were scared of. She didn't smack or beat you – often – because she knew how to wither with a glance. Even the toughest young Kray would be begging mum's forgiveness after a harsh word or two. And if – God forbid – you got in trouble with the police, or the school sent a letter home, well fifteen years' hard labour without parole would have been a birthday present compared to the tongue-lashing she dished out. Not that she wasn't capable of corporal punishment, and none of this namby-pamby bum smacking either. She might have been five foot nothing in heels, but swear in her house and she could catch you a right hook like Mike Tyson.

None of it very modern, or child-centred of course. But strangely enough, in those days you didn't have kids armed with knives and guns crawling the streets mugging people, killing each other and generally making people too scared to leave their own front door. Funny that.

Feminists

Burn the bra! Now there's a fine political gesture. Make your boobs uncomfortable for the sake of equality. You'll get no arguments from me though, love. I'll even provide the matches and hold your blouse if you promise not to turn your back. Chuck your knickers on while you're at it, we'll have a barbecue. Look, I'm getting the hang of it now; I'll stick a fork in my goolies as an expression of sympathy with the plight of the Australian aborigines.

I don't really understand how setting fire to your smalls furthers the cause. But then I don't really understand feminists. Bloody nutters the lot of them. I'll give you an example. Well-known phenomenon this. Back in the seventies when militant feminism bestrode the world like a colossus with hairy armpits, you had *heterosexual* women pretending to be *lesbians*, out of solidarity with the sisterhood. Oh well, you might say, it takes all sorts. But that's not the end of it. Those same *straight* women then started getting sniffy with *real* lesbians because they weren't doing it right. Legs weren't hairy enough, hair wasn't short enough, dungarees weren't baggy enough. Well of *course* not, you daft hetero. How are they going to pull if they go swaggering into the les-bar with their knuckles dragging along the floor looking like King Kong in a hessian sack? What cute young gay gal wants to go home with a Geoff Capes looky-likey whose underwear's still on smouldering? None, that's how many, and if you were a proper lesbian and not some man-hating pseudo-dyke you'd know it.

Now, I'm not some Neanderthal. I do miss the days when you'd come home to the smell of freshly baked knitting and a neat pile of ironed cupcakes, but you have to move with the times. I do ask this, however: if you want equality then don't pick and choose. Go all the way, love. Seems like every woman I know thinks she's a feminist, so it's funny how I never see any of them up a ladder clearing the guttering out. I've been ironing my own shirts and making my own tea since the wife read *The Female Eunuch*, but in all that time she hasn't mowed the lawn or been to the tip once. Not once. You can't switch equality on when it suits you, just like you can't *choose* to be a lesbian, so I'll tell you what; you get under the car and change the oil filter and I'll bring you out a cup of tea. Too dirty for you? Well then take that Andrea Dworkin book back to the library, put your undies back on and fire up the darning needle, my lovely.

Religious People

It's a thorny subject in this PC world where we're all too afraid of upsetting someone to speak up, but someone's got to say something about the bloody pagans. Who do they think they are with their magical chalices and ceremonial daggers? These days it's all pressure groups and lobbyists, political posturing and the taxpayer subsidising their every move. Now I've got no problem if you and Doreen the shipping clerk want to strap antlers to your heads and run around the woods in the buff, but I don't see why I should pay for it, and I don't see why I should have to read you bleating on in the press every time I open the newspaper. Oh, the nation's morals are slipping, you're badly represented in the media, all those other religions are a bit naughty … Shut up and stop trying to influence political process with your crackpot ideas.

With all due respect and deference accorded to your beliefs, I've got two words for you: The Enlightenment. Yes, I think you'll find that the Universal Life Force and State parted company some time ago, and bloody good thing too; after all, last time you lot were in charge you were burning virgins like topsy every soddin' solstice. I know, I know, it wouldn't happen now, you're all much too busy organising aromatherapy sessions and rubbing each other's chakras to go around killing innocent young women in a big wicker man. Still, you can't be too careful, can you? No, you keep your faith to the shrine in your living room and your annual pilgrimage to Stonehenge. Get Gaia involved in the business of politics and pretty soon we'll all be dancing around in our bed sheets and wearing leaves in our beards whether we want to or not, because Gaia knows what's best for us.

Immigrants

I'm talking about immigrants so you're probably already thinking I'm some nasty, brown-shirted bigot, goose-stepping around the place and voting for the British Nutter Party. Well, nothing could be further from the truth. As everyone with half an inch of brain knows, Britain is a country of mongrels. We haven't had an indigenous population since the Celt Iberians swept up from Spain, the Vikings invaded and the Normans conquered us. Over the centuries we've welcomed many peoples to our shores and wished good luck to them. Jews, Afro-Caribbeans, Asians of all sorts, millions of Australians who for some reason prefer working in some dingy London bar to sunning themselves in their own country. Anyway, occasionally there'll be another lot come knocking at the door and there may be a bit of harrumphing, but when all's said and done you shift up a bit and make room, don't you? It's just polite.

No, immigrants are all right. What sends me into a fury is all those bloody Little Britainers that look around at the black people and the brown people and the yellow people and think, 'That's it, I'm off.' Next thing you know they're all moaning on in the letters pages of the broadsheets. 'We had to leave Blighty because of the immigration. Good Lord, our culture's been overrun by Johnny Foreigner and I just didn't recognise the place any more.' And then what do they do, these bloody hypocrites? They congregate together in some lovely French village that hasn't changed since the Middle Ages, driving house prices up so the locals can't afford to live there any more, and open English shops, cricket clubs, English pubs, English schools, fish and chip shops, Conservative clubs ... They're all wandering around the place congratulating themselves on never having had to learn French in the same breath as they're moaning about never hearing English spoken in Bradford any more. And the thing that really gets me – drives me absolutely round the bloody bend – is if you ask them what they regret leaving behind in Britain, they'll sigh and tell you that they really miss a decent curry.

Do-gooders

I don't want to sound harsh, but I am, so I will. Let's be honest, you can't move for the bleeding hearts these days can you? Tambourine-botherers are pushing their little red envelopes through the door for me to fill up with my hard-earned, and earnest flip-flop jockeys are stopping me in the street to ask for a donation every time I leave the house, only these days they're not rattling a tin. Oh no. Now they're carrying direct-debit forms, the cheeky little sods. My spare change not good enough for you any more? Well up yours, then. I wouldn't give my bank details to some spotty teenager in a silly hat if my *own* life depended on it. I'd have dropped a couple of quid in a bucket to save the donkeys, but as you only deal in serious currency these days I'll buy myself a pint instead. And there's no escape. All year round they're advertising on the telly. 'Look at this poor, sweet puppy. Give us full access to your accounts immediately, or he'll die.' And then there's whole nights of guilt-trip TV. You know the kind, where you get twenty seconds of lame comedy every hour then fifty-nine minutes and forty seconds of someone who was famous twenty years ago cuddling starving children and weeping all over the shop. By the time the *Little Britain* special comes on, you're howling yourself and you've picked up the phone to pledge your life's savings.

Then a year rolls around and stone me if those kids aren't still Hank Marvin. We raised fifty bezillion quid, but it still wasn't enough to fill the poor little sausage's rice bowl. Of course, what they don't show you is the country's self-appointed ruler riding around in his new gold-plated limo and unpacking crates of Kalashnikovs, or hotels stuffed with foreign-aid workers too scared to leave because they'll get a machete up the backside. All paid for by us poor buggers who've had our heartstrings tugged by Lenny Henry.

Don't get me wrong, I don't mind giving a bit to charity, but I want to see some results. And I'm wondering if the money might be better spent elsewhere. Not a popular idea with the hand-wringers, I'll bet, but if that food shipment's not getting through then how about investing a little in some state-of-the-art weaponry. Yes, that's right, *arm* the do-gooders. You know what I'd like to see? Bob Geldof at the head of an elite do-gooder militia force, parachuting into some benighted African state and machine-gunning down the tyrant who's nicked everyone's food and sold it so he can have a wardrobe full of Prada ties, or Bono rolling in on a Comic Relief tank – with a big red nose on the front – to give some genocidal maniac a taste of his own medicine. Take out the dictators, open up their personal bank accounts, and if any other would-be tyrants start getting uppity, send in Dawn French.

Baby Boomers

When I bought my house it was sixteen pence and a bag of chips and we thought that was expensive, but blimey they've gone up a bit, haven't they? Coo. For the price of a two-bedroom terrace in Hemel Hempstead these days I could have bought Buckingham Palace when I was a nipper. And Her Majesty would've given me some change. All right, so you might have the occasional recession, but even while everyone's sobbing that they've had thirty grand knocked off the price of their six-by-four broom cupboard in Kensington, us Baby Boomers can't help feeling a bit smug.

Golden generation, you see? Brought up in the sixties when there was full employment and if you were a dustman who fancied being a photographer for *Vogue* then that was fine so long as you had a pair of Cuban-heeled boots and your own frilly shirt. Bit of a slump in the seventies, I'll grant you, but we had Slade and ELO to keep our spirits up and then Thatcher was throwing old council houses at us for shillings and the promise of another kiss in the ballot box. Plus you could buy British Rail, British Telecom, British Gas and all the rest of it for tuppence a share. All those great gifts to the nation our parents built up, ours for the taking. And didn't we do nicely while we were guzzling the world's resources with not a thought for the environment or future generations? Bloody right we did. Then to top it all, just as we're coasting in towards retirement, the biggest surge in house prices since time began. The youngsters can't afford to buy an outside toilet in the Outer Hebrides, but damn me if I'm not sitting on a property portfolio that's going to see me slobbed out on a Caribbean beach for the rest of my natural. The kids and the grandkids can worry about cleaning up my CO_2 emissions while they fight over whatever scraps of food are left on the planet. Meanwhile I've got a T-shirt printed saying, 'I'm spending the kids' inheritance.' What a laugh, eh?

I'm trying to find something to be grumpy about here, but for once I'm fogged. At a loss. Can't think of a bloody thing.

TECHNOLOGY

Computers

So you've got fed up with everyone taking the mickey because you're the only person in the world not 'online' and taking the digital plunge. The computer's out of the box and squatting on the kitchen table, taunting you with its 200-gigabyte hard drive, spankings of RAM, large cache, and multimedia readiness, whatever the bloody hell all that means. And at the bottom of the box there's a slip of paper telling you that for ecological reasons (i.e. the manufacturers are too tight to spring for the printing) the manual is now supplied on a CD. So you've slipped the CD in the stereo, expecting one of those tutorials like the wife gets for her Swahili lessons and not a bloody thing. All I want to know is where's the 'on' button.

Whatever they tell you in the shop about computers being foolproof and easy these days is a lie. An out-and-out fabrication. It might be easy if you're the kind of buck-toothed, *Star Trek* gazing, never-had-a-girlfriend wonk who uses a ZX Spectrum as a coffee mat, but for those of us who grew up in a world where the closest brush you had with technology was the bedside teas-made then it's a frightening and bewildering experience designed to give you a self-esteemectomy. Press one wrong button and you get weird message boxes popping up saying 'error: this computer will self-destruct in five seconds'. And once you've got started on the message boxes there's no stopping them. 'Do you wish to disable VirusChecker?' Now, I've no idea what the machine is on about but it's got the words 'disable' and 'virus' in it and that can't be good, right? So I'm hitting 'yes' and next thing I know little animated wasps have eaten everything on the computer and I've had to fork out to have the entire thing 'reformatted'. As soon as I get it home I've got another message box: 'Are you sure you want to delete Microsoft Windows?' Well I don't know what it is so I probably don't need it ...

I finally found out that 'multimedia ready' means I can watch the telly on it or listen to music. So that's technology, is it? Well I wouldn't have bothered if I'd known. I've already got a TV you see, and a radio. Bloody thing can't even wake me up with a cup of tea.

Email

An email is just like writing someone a letter on a typewriter, but when you've finished it you don't have to bother sticking it in an envelope or brave the herd of pensioners at the post office. You just press 'send' and whoosh, off it goes. Two seconds later it's on the recipient's computer ready to read. Bloody marvellous you might think, what a great invention. But no, email is exactly rubbish, and I will tell you why.

Writing a letter takes a little bit of time and effort. Not much time and effort, I'll grant you, but once you've factored in digging around the back of the sofa for a biro, locating stationery that you could have sworn was in the back of a drawer but has mysteriously migrated to a shoe box under the bed, and actually put the bloody letter in a letterbox it amounts to just enough that you don't want to be writing more than one or two per annum. And that's the way it should be. You don't want to come down to breakfast every day to find twenty letters from virtual strangers about the state of Marjorie's hips and how well our Stacey's doing at the massage parlour, do you? It might be fun for a day or two, but then you find you're getting through six biros a day just writing responses and scratching your head trying to think of anything beside the state of your prostate to tell them about. Same rules apply with email. Within days of starting on it you'll find some absolute bastard on Friends Reunited has passed your email address on to everyone in the world and you've suddenly got a ream of correspondence from the likes of Wilfred 'Stinky' Pithers who you haven't spoken to since you left school and for good bloody reason. He drove you round the bend then and he drives you round the bend still, only now he's a smug multi-millionaire living in LA with his third, twenty-year-old wife. 'Isn't it great that modern technology's put us back in touch?' Well frankly, Stinky, no. I couldn't give a monkey's and I've got better things to do with my time than spend six hours a day replying to gits like you.

So that's one problem with email. And then, of course, there's the spam ...

Spam

When I was a lad Spam was a tinned meat that derived its name from a contraction of 'spiced ham'. It was bloody horrible, especially when served deep-fried in batter as a Spam Fritter, but nevertheless it was British and you knew where you were with a tin of it. In the so-called twenty-first century, however, 'spam' has gone the same way as other great British words such as 'gay' and 'crack'. It's disgusting the way these trendy young people can take the brand name of this once-great British product and turn it into something all computery. You'd have thought the Spam people would take legal action.

As if emails weren't enough to cope with on their own, I'm now inundated with this new type of spam. Every day brings another 'inbox' full of discount prices on Viagra. Sometimes it seems the more I reply the more emails I get. The medicine cupboard is already bursting and the wife has developed a very peculiar gait (which reminds me – 'woody' is another one), but the spam just keeps on coming. It's as if they know just how to get to me: 'Would you like a bigger penis?' Well … now you mention it. 'Melanie would like to meet you.' I bet she would. Probably heard about my forthcoming penis enlargement. 'You've won first prize in the Dutch Euro draw.' Well blow me, perhaps I could take Melanie somewhere nice, as it happens I have a few packs of Viagra going begging. Turns out I had to go to Amsterdam to claim my winnings and pay a thousand Euros to 'secure my prize' and then they said sorry I'd lost after all and no I couldn't have my thousand euros back. And Melanie was just selling more bloody Viagra.

Still, Sheik Abdullah of Jordan needs just a small loan to tide him over then he'll make me a millionaire when he gets his throne back …

The Internet

Like everything to do with computers, the internet is a pain in the proverbial to set up, so you'll have to pay someone to come and plug it in and then watch them trying not to laugh at you when you tell them you thought a space bar was a chocolate snack. But once you're 'online' as they call it and have mastered a few basics like typing your own name and remembering how to make an '@' symbol, you're off – the world is at your slow-moving fingertips.

What a world though. Wall-to-virtual-wall freaks, idiots and weirdoes if you ask me. It's all a load of old crap. Once you've posted a few expert tips on the shedheaven.com blog, you're at a loss. I'm paying twenty quid a month for unlimited access though and nothing's going to stop me getting my money's worth, so I'm sitting in front of that screen every hour that God sends trying to find something to look at. Chance would be a fine thing. Oh, you're all right if your idea of interesting is jihadi videos, Goth dungeons or pictures of cats in wigs, but try and find something that might pique the curiosity of the average citizen and you're out of luck. The other night, for example, I joined a virtual community where my avatar grew a pair of wings and wore a hat named Susan, chatted live online with the Prime Minister of Norway, booked an overland expedition to Yemen, played poker with Chip from Utah and Suhkdeep in Malaysia and looked at pictures of Esther Rantzen with no clothes on. But is there agammykneeindampweather.org? Not bloody likely.

Internet Porn

I'm a broad-minded man who's travelled the world. Dagenham, Peckham, Sidcup, Northampton, I've been around a bit in my time and I've seen a few things that would make your hair curl. Women who aren't ladies, if you know what I mean; a few of them naturist films with the volleyball and the ping-pong; I've even slipped a custard cream into some dolly bird's garter at one of them tea-dancing clubs. Even so I was not prepared for the welter of filth that hit my screen when I visited my search engine and typed in the word 'shed'. What did I get: 'Man with large sack takes it up the shed', 'Amateur midget fretworker does it in the shed', 'six foot pine shed ready to erect', pages and pages of sickening, degraded filth. Someone ought to do something, I thought – action is clearly needed. So I fetched my credit card and steeled myself to research the extent of the problem.

Three sleepless weeks later I can tell you it's worse than I thought. In my day your blue movie was simple. You'd see some old brass leaning against a wall smoking a fag, then some punter would walk up to her.

She'd pull her skirt up a bit, giving you the vague impression that somewhere above her knees might be the top of her legs, then he'd drop his pants just enough so you could see about an inch and a half of spotty bum cleavage and that would be it, you'd just see that arse crack bobbing up and down for thirty seconds while the tart flicked fag ash into it. If you were lucky she might pull her cardigan up when she'd finished her ciggie so you could see her bra. That was pornography, and pretty bloody racy we thought it was too. You wouldn't let your wife watch it and you certainly didn't want plod to come knocking when you had the boys round and the projector set up. If only we'd known how innocent it all was. These days you see worse than that on *Question Time* and the stuff you get on the internet I can't even bring myself to speak about ... Sweating naked bodies writhing in an orgy of uncontrolled lust. Amateur lesbians, professional lesbians, attachments, saddles, threesomes, foursomes, barely legal geriatrics, underwear, unfeasibly large this and looking right up that.

They say the internet's brought the world closer, but if this is the sort of thing it's going to get up to then in my opinion the world could do with being kept apart. In separate bedrooms, with good quality flannel nightwear that provides all-over coverage.

Mobile Phones

'Hello, operator, could you get me London one-one-three please. Yes, that's right, the Cartwright residence.' That's how it used to go in the old days. Of course you'd have to wait half an hour while the workshy bint finished filing her nails and found the right cable to plug in, but you got there eventually. It was a simpler time back then though. If you wanted to make a call while you were out you found a telephone box and were happy with that. Trains were a place to sit and read the paper quietly, in pubs you chatted with your mates around the table. And then some pillock had to go and invent the mobile phone. I can remember the first ones. The size of a shopping trolley they were and if you saw some pratt dragging one down the street you thought, 'Hello, here's a right Charlie. What makes him so bloody important that he can't possibly be out of contact for five minutes while he goes to fetch a sandwich?' And of course that's what it's all about: making people feel important. What percentage of calls are really necessary? How many of them are 'Darling, it's three am, I've pranged the car on the A41, barbarian hordes are closing in and aliens are about to abduct me. Could you possibly come and pick me up?' One per cent maybe? Less? No, people don't save them for important calls, instead it's all bloody pre-pubescents waving their gadgets about so everyone can see how much 'wicked bling' they've got; respect apparently being measured these days in the number of times you get called by your chump friends during one short train journey. Little bloody sods, sucking their teeth while their phone plays tinny versions of R. Kelly then shouting, 'No, I'mmm oooon a train,' seventeen times, before hanging up. Then doing it all over again *ad infinitum*. And they have the bloody nerve to look around and roll their eyes, like it's sooo difficult being them and everyone's just demanding, demanding, demanding. I tell you what. It's annoying the crap out of me and you're obviously peeved with all the interruptions too, so why don't I take that little plastic piece of rubbish and throw it out the window? I can stand in peace and your single-parent mum doesn't have to pay £100 a month for the privilege of telling everyone you're on a train just to give you the fleeting sense that anyone gives a toss.

Texting

BFF BRB M8 CYL. No, you don't need the enigma machine, that's 'text speak' that is, for use while 'texting', which is sending short emails from one mobile phone to another mobile phone and is yet one more invention that has made the world a slightly less enjoyable place to live, all in the name of 'progress'.

All over the country you see them, morons poring over their mobiles with their thumbs going like head-banging gerbils, writing their impenetrable, dull nonsense. On trains, in their cars, in offices across the land: sixty million texts flying around every day and the typical conversation goes like this:

'LOL'
'ROFL'

'ROFLMAO'
'PMSL'
'OMG ROFLMAO PMSL 4EVA'

Inspiring, isn't it? That's the stuff to make Shakespeare proud.

It used to be that the British pub was a great social hub, a place to exchange ideas, meet people, joke and banter. These days every time I go to the pub it's like sitting in at the annual general meeting of the Society of Librarians. And why? Because every beggar is hunched over their bloody mobile with their unnaturally pumped-up thumbs tip-tapping out messages bereft of any interest or grammatical structure to morons sitting in other pubs just down the road. In some instances it's even been known for two people sitting at the same table to converse in text all night long, sitting there perfectly still and blank-faced tapping out 'LOL' and 'ROFLMAO' to each other. WTF, eh?

Computer Games

When I was a kid all we had to play with was a length of pipe, a bag of industrial fertiliser, powdered ammonia and a box of matches, but then we knew how to make our own fun in those days. We'd be on our bikes straight after breakfast and the day was wasted if the police, ambulance and fire services weren't called out at least once. You can keep your Medal of Honor, if you want to play at war you set the local dump on fire by lobbing home-made grenades at 'Skelly' Harris.

Kids nowadays wouldn't know a pipe bomb if you stuck one fizzing down the back of their drawers though. No, these days it's all computer games. As far as I can see there are four types of computer game: first you got the ones where some little animated bloke with a moustache leaps about a bit, like Freddie Mercury with his leather pants full of bees. Or there's what they call 'first-person shoot 'em ups', which involves creeping about shooting people. We used to do that too, only we called it Cowboys and Indians and it involved some very complex technology called 'sticks', 'string' and 'friends'. Then you've got the games where you have to steal cars, deal drugs, beat up prostitutes, and shoot people. It's not exactly Snakes and Ladders, but, again, that's progress for you. Interestingly, I'm looking in the paper and can't help noticing the rates for car theft, violence on women, drug and gun crime are all steadily rising, but I'm sure that's nothing to do with a generation of kiddies brought up to think that kind of thing is a way of letting your hair down.

Worst of all though are the type of games where you build your own 'civilisation'. I can see the appeal in nicking a vehicle. I really can. I made off with a milk float once and had the best two minutes of my life before the milkman caught up with me and gave me a clip round the ear. I suppose there must be some sort of satisfaction in watching Freddie Mercury jump about too, after all tens of millions of Queen fans can't all have been wrong. But for the bloody life of me I cannot understand what would make a red-blooded young British kid sit in front of a computer for months on end building a virtual civilisation. 'Oh, I'll just put a warehouse there, that will improve my mercantile rating and I can open new overseas trading routes.' What sort of way is that to spend a childhood? You want my advice on successful parenting? Throw the bloody computer in the bin and give them a bit of elastic so they can make a catapult and go and shoot some squirrels.

Call Centres

If there's one thing that drives me completely mental it's bloody lying. They call it 'spin' these days of course, but it amounts to the same thing. It just means that you're being lied to by someone who hasn't got the moral backbone to admit to themselves, or you, that they're fibbing through their teeth. You get a lot of it in government of course, and you can't expect a government to be full of conniving, lying, incompetents and not have it filter down a bit. That is why businesses these days will tell you that 'Customer service has been outsourced to the Indian subcontinent and technologically stream-lined *in order to offer our customers a better, more efficient, service.*' It's a whopper of course. A porky on the same scale as 'We're going to put big hobnailed boots on and come round to kick you in the goolies for your comfort and pleasure.'

I'd have more respect for them if they just came out and told us, 'Your phone call will be answered by Indians from now on 'cos they're virtually beggars who will work for almost nothing and we need the money – the boss goes absolutely spare if he doesn't get his six-figure weekly bonus.' Or 'We have to make sure the right people get the calls because they've only got the scripts to deal with three problems at any one time.' Instead, lies, lies, lies is all you get. And the same voice over and over again: 'If you wish to speak to someone who doesn't give a tinker's fart about you or your problem, please press one now.' Then there's the long, dragging, never-ending eon of 'hold' listening to noodling jazz that's supposed to keep you calm, but is actually raising your blood pressure with every note. It gets so bad that you're actually grateful for the relief when the mechanical bint comes back to remind you that 'Your call is important to us ...' Then to cap it all, the final insult. When someone does answer the phone, their chirpy voices begin with 'How can I help you?' Well, for a start don't keep me on hold until my death-bed and change the soddin' 'hold' music every once in a soddin' while!

A company's customer service insist their all about 'providing the best possible service to our customers' until they're blue in the face, but I'll tell you what the best possible service for your customers is, shall I? When a customer calls their local branch or shop, someone picks up the ringing phone and answers their questions. If they don't know how to answer the enquiry they walk across the office to find someone who does or call back promptly. There. It's not rocket science, is it? Of course you've got more chance of finding Joan Collins in your box of Cornflakes.

Satellite Television

The trouble with satellite television is there's just too bloody much of it. I remember the good old days when it was BBC1, BBC2 and ITV. Mary Whitehouse was kind enough to make sure that you never saw any smut and of a Saturday evening you could settle down with a Vesta curry and an easy choice between *Match of the Day*, a documentary about eels and *3-2-1* with Ted Rogers and Dusty Bin. And they were considerate enough to make sure the football finished just in time for you to switch over and see a pensioner from Wolverhampton winning a speedboat and a commemorative plastic dustbin. It was good enough for us, but like everything else they had to go and muck it up. First you had la-di-da Channel 4 showing wall-to-wall filth for 'intellectuals', then Channel 5 lowered the already crumbling standards to a point where you thought things couldn't get any worse. But that was just the beginning. Suddenly satellite dishes, sprouted like tumours from every pebble-dashed semi in the country – wrecking the aesthetics of British architecture, incidentally – and finding something you want to watch is like finding a *Big Brother* winner still with TV career.

You can spend hours going up and down the channels, trying to find a decent show among the endless repeats of *Friends, A House in the Sun* and bloody *Extreme Makeover* and by the time you've found something it's just finishing, so you end up watching *Most Haunted* yet again, hating yourself for getting caught up with a bunch of feeble-minded hoaxers and an ex-*Blue Peter* presenter pushing a glass round the table. 'Are there any spirits here?' Exactly right, Yvette. After five minutes of *Most Haunted* I'm hitting the Scotch every time.

And what's all this red button 'interactive' nonsense all about, huh? I don't want to interact with the telly any more than I want to stick my privates in the toaster. I'm paying through the nose to be entertained so stop wasting my money on stupid red buttons – and that Simon Cowell while I'm on the subject – and bring back some good-quality programming like *Catchphrase*.

Sport

Cricket

Cricket, now that *used* to be a sport. A tactical masterclass of chess on grass played out over five glorious days while you sat and watched from your deckchair, getting wonderfully squiffy on something fruity and alcoholic, occasionally waking from your afternoon nap to discover that after two and a half days, Geoffrey Boycott was still to get off the mark.

And then the marketing men got hold of it. The idiots in bright ties decided that no one can concentrate for five days any more, so they came up with the idea of the one-day match instead. And when they got bored of that – a whole day? Sitting in the sunshine watching cricket? Heaven forbid – they invented 'Twenty20', in which each side get twenty overs and the match is over in a couple of hours. Hey, why stop there? Why not have one over a side? Why not have a single ball each. Heck, why bother with the cricket at all – let's just flip a coin and be done with it. We could call it the toss match, in your honour.

If messing with the format wasn't enough for the marketing 'maestros', they got their fashion friends in and decided that wearing cricket whites was a bit old-fashioned. So out went the classic cricket clothes that people have been wearing for centuries and in came, well … pyjamas. Yellows and Blues and Greens and Purples –

it's enough to make your eyes hurt, particularly after several hours of drinking in the sun. And if that wasn't enough, they decided that the one thing on the cricket pitch that wasn't white – the ball – should now be white instead. Brilliant.

Then there are the names. Another 'bright spark' has obviously sat there and gone 'Hey! Has anyone noticed cricket is a bit like baseball? Why don't we give them silly names like they do in the USA?' Yes, what a fantastic idea. As if the format and the kit wasn't enough, let's saddle the teams with stupid nicknames as well. That's *bound* to pull the punters in. So now we've got the Essex Eagles and the Lancashire Lightning and the Surrey Brown Caps. I wish I was making this up.

At least they could have made a stab at getting the names to match up with the counties, rather than just let them be computer generated. Why the Yorkshire Carnegie, when it should be the Yorkshire Tight Bastards? Why not the Surrey Commuters and the Essex Girls and the Somerset Farmers?

Honestly, it's just not cricket.

Kick off Times

Call me a bit of a traditionalist, but I like my football matches to start at three o'clock on a Saturday afternoon. It's part of the fabric of the British weekend – football at three o'clock on a Saturday afternoon, church on a Sunday morning. But then television turned up and thought they could do it all a bit better. So now, we've got matches on Saturday lunchtime, when *Football Focus* is still gamely trying to preview something that has already started, Saturday evening, when you're having your tea, Sunday lunch when you're having your roast, and Sunday afternoon when you're out for a walk. There's more league games on Monday night, Champions League on Tuesday and Wednesday, UEFA Cup on Thursday, Championship on a Friday, then the whole charade starts all over again. Give it a couple of years and they'll be scheduling matches in the middle of the night so the American 'fanbase' can have their mealtimes interrupted too. You think I'm joking? You've obviously never stayed up until 4 am to watch a boxing match.

And they all get so excited about their matches the whole time. Grand Slam Sunday? I don't know which marketing numpty came up with that – and let's face it, it's always some idiot from marketing – but all of a sudden everyone's wetting themselves because someone's fixed the fixture list so the 'Big 4' (The Big Four? Don't get me started) can play back to back. Grand Slam Sunday? What do you think this is? Basketball? God only knows what they've got up their sleeves next: Death Match Monday? Showdown Saturday? Well Hard Wednesday? Here's a couple of ideas of my own – how about Football Free Friday? And Correct Kick off Time With No Television Cameras Allowed Saturday.

Football Cheats

Sometimes when you are watching a game of football, it is necessary to remind yourself that our national sport is actually football, and not in fact diving. Because these days, it seems impossible for a professional footballer to stay on their feet longer than five minutes. All it takes is a glance from an opposition player, and down they go like they're JFK and someone has just taken a pot shot at them from the Book Depository.

My God, you think, this does look serious. Are they going to pull through? I wonder how long it will be before they're able to walk again? Let me tell you how long it'll be before they are able to walk again – about ten seconds or so, once the referee has given the penalty and sent the innocent defender off for an early bath.

I don't want to sound like we were made of sterner stuff in my day, but ... actually, that's exactly what I want to sound like. When I went to watch the football with my dad back in the eighteenth century or whenever it was, football pitches were like mudbaths, and balls were so soggy and heavy that they dented your face if you tried to head one. And a tackle was a tackle. Studs up, full-blooded and meaty. But did anyone complain? Good golly gosh they didn't. You didn't have substitutes in those days – players just had to get up and hobble on. And that's exactly what they did. Anyone who tried play-acting would quickly find out what it felt like to feel a proper tackle.

It would be easy to say that the arrival of diving coincided with the influx of foreign players into the league, but let's be honest, there's more than enough home-grown divers out there these days to make you feel ashamed to be British. I blame the large amounts of cash these namby-pamby players trouser to turn up and fall over. No living in digs with chops for tea and lights out by ten for this lot. Just swanning around from nightclub to nightclub, six-figure cheque to six-figure cheque.

You know how I'd sort it out? Have a surgeon ready by the side of the pitch. Then the next time one of these divers takes a tumble, screaming and crying how they're never going to walk again, let the referee say, 'You're right, the only thing for it is a life-saving operation,' then get the surgeon on to perform an instant amputation. That'll stop the little sod putting it on in future.

England

Of course, in the old days, we used to be world champions at football. Quite right too, we invented the bloody game, so it only stands to reason that we should be hoisting the trophy on a regular basis. But apart from 1966, what has the England football team got to put in their trophy cabinet? Sweet FA. As cupboards go, it's about as bare as Katie Price on a photoshoot.

Personally, I think the rot started with the FA Board, for failing to give the manager's job to Cloughie. He'd have sorted everyone out with a clip round the ear. Now we're resigned to giving the job to Johnny Foreigner, people like Sven who was so focussed on the job, he could be found hard at work with his secretary. It says something when the best English candidate for the job is Steve McClaren, the self-styled 'wally with the brolly', who can't even qualify for the major tournaments.

And when we do get there, it's always the same old formula – play desperately badly against no-hope teams, and then get beat by the first half-decent side we come across in the tournament, usually on penalties. Now, I don't know about you, but is it really that difficult to get the ball in the back of the net from twelve yards? Every other country in the world seems to manage it, but all we can do is blast the ball into outer space (yes, Chris Waddle, I'm talking to you) or fall over while taking the kick (David 'Divot' Beckham, you're a disgrace).

I think we should start a campaign to do away with penalties and come up with another way of settling a match instead, one that our footballers have more of a chance of winning. How about a competition to see who can pull and throw up over a 'lady' first? Or who can urinate into a pint glass because we can't be bothered to go to the nightclub toilet? Or beat up the person in front of you in the queue at McDonald's because he looked at you funny? Suddenly, the Germans and Italians wouldn't look so confident after all. And we'd be, quite literally, world-beaters all over again.

Sport in the Media

Here's how sport used to work: sportsmen would play until they were thirty, then they'd retire and run a pub. That way, the nation had fond memories of their sporting prowess, held firmly intact by the fact that we never bumped into their ugly mug ever again.

These days, though, no sooner are the buggers off the pitch before they're in the television studio, with their new-fangled 'media' career as a 'pundit' or (you have to laugh at this) 'analyst'. Just because you've managed to squeeze your frame into a shirt and tie, Sonny Jim, does not mean that you are the sporting equivalent of a banker or financial whiz kid. You're not an analyst; you're a has-been, clinging on to the limelight for dear life. And every numbskull utterance you make erases every golden memory we have of your time on the pitch.

Not that the commentators are much better. My God, 'They Think It's All Over … It Is Now', feels like Shakespeare compared to some of the garbage that the new breed of commentators feel obliged to spout. All of them seem to speak in that way of the English abroad – they think that by SHOUTING, they'll somehow get their point across. The only point it actually gets across, of course, IS THAT YOU DON'T KNOW WHAT YOU'RE TALKING ABOUT.

I'll tell you who are the worst, though: the fans. In the old days, they used to been seen and not heard: now they've got their own talk shows and phone-ins where they can witter on to their heart's content. *You've Heard The Match, You've Listened to the Managers, Now It's Your Turn* … No, it's not. Now it's your turn … to go down the pub if you want a moan because none of the rest of us give a rat's arse about what you've got to say.

You see, if only the ex-player went into the pub industry, the fans would have somewhere to go and moan, and the ex-player would have an audience to listen to their 'expert' views. And the rest of us could enjoy a bit of peace and quiet.

Tennis

Tennis. Now that's a load of crap these days. And I don't just mean the English players, even though they have been utter trousers for as long as you can remember. Come on, Tim? How about Come Off It, Tim, No One Seriously Expects You To Win. Then there was that guy from Canada who looked like a horse, who obviously decided to pretend to be 'English' to cover the fact that he couldn't actually win. Now we've got that lad from Scotland who has more chance of hitting puberty than a decent cross-court volley. Fred Perry, where are you now?

No, what gets me about tennis is how *dull* the game has become. Gone are the days of wooden rackets, where you had to have a bit of skill to win a match. Now you've got scientifically sprung graphite lite ubersmart rackets with bigger heads (isn't that cheating?) that ping the ball so fast, the opponent doesn't have a chance of getting the 150mph serve back. The only tension in the men's game these days is whether the guy is going to serve an ace or a double fault.

Obviously, for a red-blooded man such as myself, the women's game holds a bit more interest, particularly all those Russians, Olivia WhyDon'tYouPopOver or whatever their names are. But just as things are getting interesting, up pops the bloody British weather, and your lovely daydream about Natalia Legover is interrupted by the sight of Cliff Richard 'serenading' the Centre Court, with his selection of classic hits. God only knows what the rest of the world are thinking. Or Sue Barker for that matter.

And as usual, technology is there, sticking its nose in where it isn't wanted. Back in the days, you'd have chalk dust and dodgy line calls, and John McEnroe going absolutely ballistic in disbelief that his serve wasn't in. Obviously that was far too much fun for the paying public, so someone invented a machine that goes 'beep' instead when the ball is out, and no one is allowed to ever argue with it. Well that'll bring the crowds flocking back, won't it? And they wonder why Britain doesn't produce tennis champions any more.

Competitive Dads

Of course, for some people, watching the beautiful game isn't quite enough. And though they can't actually take part themselves, they can do the next best thing: make their sons take part instead.

No matter that Little Johnny has two left feet, and would far rather be at home killing things on his Playstation. As far as his dad is concerned, he could be the next George Best, and so it's down to the playing fields bright and early on a Saturday morning to take part in something approaching a football game.

Of course, Little Johnny is nowhere near being the next George Best, a fact that his Dad reinforces by standing on the touchline and swearing and shouting at him until he is blue in the face. If Little Johnny didn't care much for football at the start of the game, by the end he is going to hate the game for ever.

Sometimes Little Johnny is so bad that the only way he is going to get in the football team is if his dad agrees to take over as coach. And if Little Johnny isn't the next George Best, then his dad is most certainly not the new Bill Shankly either, whatever he might think. There is no more pathetic sight than a grown man living his fantasy of being a top football coach, and attempting to drill complicated team formations into a group of boys who don't know one end of the pitch from the other.

I was lucky that my dad wasn't too pushy in this regard – he saw that I was better at watching football than playing it, and the one time he came to watch me on a freezing cold morning, he took me aside at half time with a small piece of advice – 'next time that winger tries to go past you, son, kick him'. Two minutes into the second half I kicked him so hard that I got sent off, which meant me and my dad could bugger off to the café for a cup of tea and a bacon sandwich. He was smart like that, my dad.

Running A Marathon

Who the hell invented jogging as a pastime? Man moves at two speeds – running and walking: this half-arsed middle way in badly fitting tracksuit bottoms (and they're always badly fitting) is simply not a sport. It's a sweaty stroll round the park without allowing yourself time to take in the view. Not that it stops the eejits thinking that they're Rocky Balboa, wheezing their way up the park steps with 'Eye of the Tiger' blaring out of their I-Pod.

Of course, some of these joggers don't leave it there. Oh no, they have to go the whole hog and run a marathon, don't they? Which would be fine by me – one less person in the post office queue – except they can't stop going on about it. How they're 'in training'. How they're worried they haven't got enough 'miles under their belt'. How they're suffering from 'jogger's nipple'. I tell you what, bore me with your story about 'hitting the wall' one more time, and you'll be suffering from jogger's nipple all right.

But even lording it over the rest of us about how they're uberhuman for running what is a fairly random distance (26 miles and a few hundred yards?) is not enough. No, the smug show-offs have to combine their keep-fit fanaticism with the utter worthiness of doing it for charity. *Yah, I'm running dressed as a Giant Gorilla in order to, like, save the Giant Gorilla.* And of course, if you don't sponsor their sweaty arse for at least a pound a mile, then everyone in the office thinks you're a right tight bastard.

Let me tell you this – you might think you're better than me, but you're not. Have I ever pulled down my trousers and taken a poo by the side of the road? No, Paula Radford, I haven't. And should I do so, I would expect to be rightly castigated by society for a serious affront to civilisation. Paula, though, remains a national hero. It's absolute madness. And it put me right off my custard creams for a week, too.

So the next time someone asks you why you've never run a marathon, just tell them that you're not stupid enough to put yourself in a position where you have to crap in the street. We non-marathon runners may not have a medal to show for our efforts, but we have something far more important. It's called dignity.

Extreme Sports

I'll tell you what else really gets my goat. People who aren't happy with just playing football or cricket or rugby or tennis, but have to go one better – who have to take part in what they consider an 'extreme' sport.

I'm not really sure what an extreme sport is – I think it basically involves taking a traditional game, golf for example, and sticking the word 'extreme' in front of it: voila! Welcome to the world of extreme golf. How you play this 'extreme' version is, as far as I can work out, to completely ignore all the rules that made the sport in the first place. So extreme golfers, rather than potter pleasantly around a lush green course for 18 holes, before retiring to the club bar for a refreshing half of shandy, decide they would rather bash their golf ball around a desert instead. Or the Arctic. There was even one guy who decided to hack his way from one side of Mongolia to the other. The mind, quite frankly, boggles.

What's next? Extreme football, played in a minefield? Extreme cricket, using crocodiles for bats? Why can't these morons be satisfied with the simple pleasures of playing a classic game that has been around for centuries? Personally, I think it's time that the rest of us stopped indulging the extremists into thinking that they are somehow harder and more adventurous than the rest of us, and rebranded their 'extreme' sports as 'twat' ones instead. I'll wager that the take-up in 'twat golf' will disappear overnight, leaving the most extreme parts of the sport being the decision to use a four iron to get out of the bunker.

Boxing

Boxing – a great British sport, great British tradition. One only has to witness the punch-up in the taxi ranks at chucking-out time to realise that as a nation, we all have the ability to throw a strong hook … and miss.

That's my problem with modern British boxers. They keep on bloody winning. Joe Calzaghe, Ricky Hatton and the rest, where's the fun in being world champion? Aren't they aware of the long-standing British role of getting royally thumped? By not giving in to the American pretender, they are throwing the whole boxing world out of order.

Henry Cooper, now there was a boxer. Knew how to take a punch, knew how to fall down, knew when to slap on a bit of Brut for the cameras. Frank Bruno, too: we all saw that one punch he threw at Mike Tyson – one punch that Tyson responded to by knocking seven shades of crap out of him. The thing is, that as long as there were people out there fighting for Blighty and losing, there was still the chance that you might just be the hardest person in the country.

But with Calzaghe and Hatton flooring all before them, that simple daydream which should be a required right for every red-blooded male is blown away instead. One only has to watch a few minutes of 'The Hitman' to realise that, actually, we wouldn't stand a chance. Instead, we can only conclude that we are the washed-up has-been we really are, who is in no way a proper contender. Can dent a man's confidence, that, no end.

GREAT BRITAIN

The North

As a whole, on balance, and with all things taken into account, it's a bloody marvellous country is your Great Britain. We've got pubs, we've got pork pies *and* scratchings, more curry houses in Barnsley alone than there are on the Indian subcontinent, we've got Jeremy Clarkson, Ann Widdecombe, Her Majesty the Queen, *Strictly Come Dancing*, fields full of cows with hardly a touch of CJD, and there will always be a fresh pair of knockers on page three of the *Sun* each and every day of the year. That's a given. And if that little lot doesn't make a country world-class then I don't know what does. Nevertheless, every so often you come across a little pocket, just a tiny area, that lets the side down. I'm referring – of course – to the North.

As you drive up the M1, or inch your way up the M1 at the speed of a one-legged, asthmatic tortoise, there's a distinct feeling that it's all getting gloomier with every passing mile. You must have noticed. First of all there's that rusty pile of scrap iron that looks like someone's jammed the skeleton of a B52 bomber into the ground arse first, then come Blake's dark, satanic mills pouring filth over the landscape and there you are. The North. It's like Mordor on a wet weekend.

Not their fault. No one could say that the northerners are to blame. It's just one of those sad accidents that it ended up a place apart, full of wizened and depressed little gnomes in dirty macs with flat caps and flat beer, sucking on a pathetic roll-up while hunched over a copy of the *Racing Post*, with a pigeon tucked in their breast pocket and a ferret loose in their drawers. And that's just the ladies.

It used to be all right up there when they had their steel mills and their shipyards and whatnot all banging away. You wouldn't want to visit, but they were getting along and no ideas above their station. Then it all went to pot and while the rest of the country raced ahead the North flopped around like a suicidal halibut. You'll occasionally see them trying to make a fist of it; putting up a flash new bridge in Newcastle or advertising Sheffield as a happening, chic city. Pushing their Roy 'Chubby' Browns and Jimmy Nails as quality entertainers. It's all a bit embarrassing though, like that one guest at the party who's trying to dance even though he just split up with his girlfriend on the day his dog died and he got made redundant. You have to feel a little bit sorry, but that doesn't mean you'll go over and talk to the miserable beggar.

The South

Mind you, where the North might be a bit grim at least it's not full of pretentious la-di-das like the South, with their carefully fringed 'do's', Hennes scarves and a perfectly groomed Chihuahua in their fake Louis Vuitton clutch bag. Plucked, waxed, botoxed and manicured until they look like a shop dummy, then slathered in creosote some cosmetic company's had the gall to call 'self-tan' and flog for fifty quid a square inch. And that's just the blokes. Bunch of condescending mung bean-munching metrosexuals, the lot of them.

What's so bloody great about the South? That's what I want to know. All right they've got London, but let's unpack that a little bit shall we? 'London's a great city,' they all squeal, the southerners. 'It's all *shiny* and *cosmopolitan* and, well, you can see *We Will Rock You* at the Dominion Theatre.' Cosmopolitan? Do me a favour. Unless of course your idea of cosmopolitan is being mugged every two yards, £3.50 for a paper cup of weak tea and every shop selling tourist tat with a Union Jack printed on it. There are nice places in London, I'll grant you. They belong to non-doms and sleazy City fat cats and are tucked away behind huge fences. Either that or they're overrun with Americans who'll stop you every two seconds to ask the way to Lie-sester Square and which tube line to take for Stonehenge*. No, London is a cesspit and the rest of the South is no better. Prove it? Gentlemen of the jury, I give you Slough, Basingstoke, Woking, Dagenham, Milton Keynes, Watford and Southampton.

Case for the prosecution rests, m'lud.

*Stonehenge? That'll be the Circle Line my trans-Atlantic friend. It'll take a while, but be patient and you'll get there eventually.

Scotland

No reasonable person could deny that the Sweaty Socks have made a contribution over the years. The country's produced great engineers, actors, writers and statesmen. In Billy Connolly they've got one of the finest banjo players that the British Isles has to offer and they even have their own monster: Gordon Brown. They are undoubtedly the world's gingerest nation and are also speeding impressively up the fattest chart having pioneered the deep-fried Cadbury's Crème Egg – no mean achievement in itself for a country whose only other gift to world cuisine is minced sheep and turnips stuffed into a stomach lining.

So, why is it that I'd rather pour piranhas into my Y-fronts than venture north of the border? Well, frankly, it's because I know where I'm not wanted. No other region in the history of the world has despised its closest neighbours so much as the Scots hate the English. Oh, they'll attempt to maintain a veneer of friendliness, but as soon as they've had one drink – which will be just after they get up in the morning – the bile will start dribbling out and after a few more 'wee drams' it'll be a tsunami of hatred for anyone who hails from south of the border. They'll dredge up ancient feuds over Skipping Prince Wullie and relive the Battle of Bollockburn. They'll wax lyrical about some old vagrant who lived in a cave and ate spiders and they'll bang on endlessly about Mel Gibson. None of it of any interest to your average English person, of course, because it all happened years ago and even if English schools still bothered to teach British History no one down south would really give a mouse's fart about it any more. I mean, give it a rest already, Jock. No one likes a bad loser, but especially when they're still moaning on and on about how they was robbed six hundred years after the fact.

So, my philosophy *vis-à-vis* the Scottish is this: you go and climb into your dress with the furry manbag hanging off the front and I'll stay down here where it rains just ever so slightly less and pray for the day they dissolve the union. And after the Jocks have gone, I can start praying for the Taffies to bugger off.

Rudeness

Now, I'm no prude, but I do miss Mary Whitehouse. A lovely lady – God rest her – and a champion of morality. Someone needs to stand up for a bit of bloody decency and civility in this country and since Mary passed on standards haven't so much declined as curled up their toes completely. On a scale of one to ten, with ten being 'Good morning, sir' and one being 'Up yours, grandpa', we're now at about minus twenty-six, or 'What are you ******* looking at you old ****.' Filth and swearing and downright bloody rudeness, it's everywhere. You switch on the telly and it's effing this and blinding that. And that's just *Blue Peter*. After the watershed it gets even worse, I keep expecting the next BBC costume drama to be called Knickerless Bonkelby. You go into a shop and no one will meet your eye, let alone say 'hello' and if you give them a smile you'd think you'd just jumped up and down on their privates singing Hare Krishna. Open the door for a lady and she'll stick her nose in the air. You'd need to stick hot needles under her fingernails for a 'thank you' and even then you'd get it in a sarky tone. Shop assistants huff and puff at you if you dare to waste their texting time by trying to buy something and customer services don't want to provide any service. No, they just want you out of their faces as quickly as possible, preferably with a flea in your ear so you'll think twice before trying their patience again.

A bit of common bloody courtesy, it's all I ask. It never cost anyone anything. Whereas, if anyone tells me to 'talk to the hand' one more bloody time it could cost them their front teeth.

Plumbers

Somewhere in Britain there is a secret school all plumbers attend. But it doesn't teach them how to plumb. Oh no. Its courses include, Advanced Procrastination; Making Money, Drinking Tea; Text Your Way to a Fortune; Stop Yourself Laughing as You Write out the Invoice; and – of course – the ever popular, Employing a Teenage Greasy-Haired Nitwit who Will Screw Everything Up so You Can Charge Even More Money to Put it Right.

I know this school exists because no matter how many times I work my way through the Yellow Pages looking for a British plumber with even a shred of mercy the scenario remains the bloody same. It starts with a leaky pipe. Annoying, but not too bad. It's dripping down the walls and needs looking at *tout suite* or it's going to wreck the carpet. With a sigh and a curse, I'll pull out the phone book, close my eyes and stick a pin in at random. Then, deciding that Balloon Animal Pete, Children's Party

Entertainer probably won't be able to help, I'll try again with my eyes open and pick out 'Honest Dan's Totally Honest Plumbing Service', setting the following train of events in motion:

Honest Dan will arrive two hours late and expect a hot cup of tea to be waiting for him. There will follow a fifteen-minute getting-to-know-you session in the kitchen after which he will expect his mug to be refilled.

HD's mobile phone will ring, leading to a forty-five-minute conversation with his (specially primed) wife. Dan will lounge around the kitchen chatting to the missus and occasionally waggle his eyebrows and empty mug at you.

Noticing you looking at the clock HD will reluctantly ring off and say, 'Women, eh? They do go on,' just in time for another cup of tea and a bit of a chinwag before getting down to work.

An hour and a half after arriving HD will poke his head into the attic for all of three seconds then return to tell you that you have a leaky pipe. Now it's time for tea and a serious chat about your options. He could bodge it for now, of course, but the rest of it's going to go soon so you should really get him and 'the boy' to replace it. If you agree he'll stop the leak, if you don't he'll suck his breath in and tell you you'll need to get another plumber then, because he likes 'to do a job properly'.

After you've agreed to replace all the pipework, HD will climb into the attic, put a bit of tape round the pipe and come down to prepare your invoice for the evening's work. Because he's 'Honest' Dan he's knocked ten minutes off the price because he took that phone call earlier, leaving you to pay just an hour and fifty minutes for his time, plus call-out charge and materials. A snip at £450.

Two weeks later he and 'the boy', who appears to have been raised in the wild by stoats, will arrive and totally bugger your house up while drinking more tea than you would have believed the human body capable of. Then charge you the equivalent of the GDP of Luxembourg.

And that's why I love immigrants. You won't catch me moaning about the Poles. No-siree. I'm holding welcoming parties at Stansted airport. I'm hugging them round the knees as they come out of arrivals with tears of gratitude in my eyes.

The Seaside

It used to be lovely, the Great British seaside. All beautifully trimmed ornamental gardens and brass bands, saucy postcards and granddad lying in his deckchair with a hanky knotted round his head. Great days those were, letting the young ladies have a nibble on your cockles or a suck of your rock. And you didn't mind if it rained a bit because The Only Slightly Racist Show would be packing them in on the pier, and who didn't enjoy watching those blokes running around with boot polish on their faces and giving it the old jazz hands.

A great British tradition, your summer jaunt to the beach, and where's it gone, hey? Now it's all video-game arcades, beaches covered in broken alcopop bottles and a couple of turds bobbing around in the sea – probably called Wayne and Dwayne. The only good thing about the seaside is that they'll probably get hypothermia or some vicious disease from all the effluent in the water. And they have *nudist* beaches. I kid you not. Actual beaches where dirty perverts go naturist and no one comes to arrest them. In Britain! No word of a lie, I took the wife down to Brighton last summer. It was a lovely day so we had an afternoon nap on the front and woke up with some dolly bird standing in front of us with no knickers on. Everything hanging out for all to see. Now, I'm a stickler for tradition me. I'm at the British seaside and I've seen the postcards, so I know exactly what to say. 'Lawks, Nelly,' I shouted, 'What a lovely pair of jellies. Have you got crabs, too?'

After she'd finished beating me round the head with her Birkenstocks I vowed I'd never go back to the British seaside again.

Theme Parks

Why do they call them 'theme' parks? What's the bloody 'theme'? Queuing? Being jostled all day by fat, tattooed inbreds from Scunthorpe? Or, could it possibly be ripping people off? Go to Thorpe Towers Sticklebrick World of Fun or whatever and you're almost guaranteed a heart attack before you even get through the turnstile. The grandkids have had to wrestle me to the ground and sit on me while the wife jemmies the wallet out of my hands with a crowbar to pay the Have-a-Nice-Day girl the equivalent of a fortnight in Bermuda.

So I'm not in a good mood before we've even started and the last thing I want to see is some drama school dropout pirouetting in front of me dressed as Squirrel bloody Nutkin. As far as I'm concerned it's adding insult to injury. Nevertheless, the family's dragged me away before I've committed GBH and now we're off to enjoy the park's famous attractions, first of which is the Fiery Terminator rollercoaster. Now, if they were being strictly truthful it should just be called the Insanely Boring Queue, because you'll be there for an hour before you even get a sniff of your thirty-second ride. And then what? It's not a rollercoaster, it's a holding-you-upside-down-and-shaking-you-until-all-the-money-falls-out machine. I swear I looked down to see some bloke sweeping up all the cash that had fallen out of people's pockets.

Next up on the itinerary will be making your way to the next ride. A scene that I imagine bears resemblance to the Israelites crossing the Red Sea. It's a chaos of tangled arms and limbs and baby buggies, shoving and swearing with another hour in a queue to look forward to at the end of it. So, two rides in and half the day's gone. It's time to stand behind fifty more fat families who want to order everything on the menu while you wait for your fast-food lunch, which for some reason is double the price it is on the high street. After that you won't be able to face another hour in a queue again quite yet so you'll try one of the attractions where you only have to queue for half an hour. Oh dear. It's a miniature train that will puff and tremble around the park, offering a superb view of the gravel pit next door, until it drops you at the zoo. If you can describe a selection of sheds with a depressed-looking donkey and a vicious llama as a zoo.

By now it's mid-afternoon, and you'll be clutched with a burning need to *get your money's worth*, so it's back to standing in line for the opportunity to be thrown around like a cat in a spin dryer. There's no chance though. Two more rides and they'll be herding you out through the gift shop where the grandkids will be on your case for fluffy biros and novelty hats. The average cost per ride was twenty-three quid, not including a lunch that everyone threw up anyway, ice creams, gifts and a photograph of yourself soiling your pants on The Deathtrap.

Castles, Stately Homes and Other Historic Attractions

In my opinion, if you've seen one big house stuffed to the rafters with Americans you've seen them all. But occasionally the wife will be gripped with a desire to go and look at some tumbledown old hovel in the middle of nowhere. And as it's that or a weekend on my knees waging the War on Weeds I'll agree to spend six hours in the car with some wilted sandwiches and a bottle of warm pop while we crawl across the country to a National Trust Landmark that looks like every other National Trust Landmark. Dull portraits of dead rich people? Check. A four-poster that Archibald the Forgettable once slept in? Check. Forty-year-old 'animatronic' dummy that moves its squeaky arm up and down while dressed in period clothes? Check. Tinny harpsichord music? Check. Two-foot high 'maze' that a dwarf with learning difficulties couldn't get lost in? Check. Disgruntled aristo owner who now lives in the attic because the family can't afford the upkeep any more? Check.

I don't get the attraction myself, but the missus loves it. One glimpse of a peacock strutting across the lawn and you'd think she'd died and gone to Hampton Court. Still, there's worse I suppose. No matter how dull your average stately home is it's got nothing on the 'Is That It?' factor of some of your other British landmarks. Naming no names, but have you ever been to the Hellfire Caves in West Wycombe? Sounds exciting, you might think, and yes the caves come complete with a history of devil worship, dark orgies and *murder*. Got to be worth a visit, eh? But you'll spend three hours on the M40 to find that the West Wycombe Caves are smaller than your average rabbit warren and have all the atmosphere of a Harvester restaurant. The only murder likely to be committed was when I found out I'd paid a tenner to enter the bowels of the earth only to find out I was in someone's bloody underground box room with yet another bleeding animatronic dummy waving at me.

Mind you, even the West Wycombe Caves look like an entrancing land of wonder and thrills next to the disappointment that is Stonehenge. It's some rocks. Some of them balanced on top of others. Excuse me if I don't wet my pants in excitement.

Litter and Graffiti

Everywhere you go in Britain these days there's plastic bags blowing like tumbleweed down the streets, discarded cans of Tennent's Extra with their accompanying pavement pizza – which you won't notice until it's too late because you're ankle-deep in fast-food packaging – old sofas peeking out of hedgerows and every available surface covered in the scrawlings of teenage glue heads. I think it's safe to say that, as a species, the Womble of Wimbledon Common is now extinct. Probably the first of God's creatures to have been wiped out by overtime.

What is it that makes the British, as a nation, incapable of putting rubbish in the bin? You see people standing right next to perfectly functional, completely empty litter receptacles. It's right there. All they have to do is put their hand out and drop their burger box in. Laboratory rats could learn to do it, but it's completely beyond the intellectual grasp of the majority of UK citizens. No, they'd rather drop it to the floor, sneer at anyone who watches them do it and start a knife fight if you dare ask them to pick it up. And we let them get away with it! To my mind there should be a stiffer penalty for littering: something with a Roman flavour, perhaps involving lions, would be appropriate *and* make a more enjoyable family day out than Alton bloody Towers.

Now littering gets me upset. Seeing people dropping rubbish makes me want to take one of those sticks with a point on the end and ram it up their backside. Sideways. But my fury over littering pales beside my incandescent rage at those people – yes, the bloody hand-wringers again – who think graffiti is an art form. Apparently we shouldn't be giving young Tyler (or Tagz, as he likes to sign his works) six of the best, a bucket of soapy water and a scrubbing brush. Oh no, we should be giving him a *grant*. Don't stifle the little darling's talent, *pay* him to spray over even more of our once green and pleasant public spaces with his narcissistic, adolescent drivellings. Now, I must admit, I'm not an art connoisseur, but I'm pretty certain that great art doesn't involve daubing a willy and the word 'Tagz' on every available surface within a ten-mile radius, including motorway bridges. I don't recall Botticelli spraying 'Bottyz' all over Renaissance Europe or Da Vinci painting the Mona Penis fifty foot high on the side of the Louvre in garish colours with a wonky head. No, they used canvases, which is what you do when you're an artist. If they painted willies at all, they would be discreet, understated willies and certainly not gushing fluids.

One of these nights I'm going to every bridge along the M6 with a bucket of extra-slippery oil. Then I'm going to take the wife for a drive. 'Oh look, dear,' I'll say. 'It's raining vermin. I'd better put the windscreen wipers on.'

Industrial Estates

Is there anything more soul-destroying than a British industrial estate? Any place on earth more wretchedly miserable than a conglomeration of corrugated-iron shacks squatting at the edge of town, spewing out forklift trucks and shrink-wrapped pallets? Populated by drifting wraiths. Despondent, blank-eyed fugitives from a Lowry painting who only have to look around themselves for a constant reminder that their career never really took off, because no one, ever, *chooses* to work on an industrial estate; a place with no pubs, no cafés, no shops at all – just a sandwich man who cycles round once a day, shuddering at the horror of it all. Even the bosses will be broken. Back in the day it was all going to take off. Manufacturing and warehousing could stay in the estate, but he and the design and sales teams were going to have plush offices uptown. He'd be able to hand his business card out with aplomb at Lodge meetings, secure in the knowledge that the address line didn't read 'Unit Two, Dogcrap Industrial Estate.' Somehow though, it never happened. Oh, they struggle along, but the market for the design and print of company brochures and letterheads isn't what it was, what with the internet and everything, and all his dreams of a nationwide chain have shrunk to twelve employees approaching retirement age and a patch of concrete with weeds growing between the cracks. And he wouldn't have that if some of the other masons hadn't taken pity and given him a few orders.

The architects might make a half-hearted attempt to make the industrial estate seem all right, an exciting, dynamic hub of enterprise even, especially with the newer ones. But it won't be their best work. After all, what famous architect is remembered for his industrial estates? And besides, the budget is tight. The posher ones might even go so far as planting a few shrubs and trees, which will never get to more than two foot high – nobody knows why for sure, but it's probably depression – and choose a grand-sounding name like Manorfields International Commercial Park. Get through the gates though and it's always just another bunch of prefabs, but now with the addition of a sad, duckless pond off to one side.

At the end of the day, no matter how hard the architects and landscapers try, there will be no disguising that a British industrial estate is just a graveyard of broken dreams.

ABROAD

The British Empire

Those were the days. Britain was the Land of Hope and Glory and a fifth of the globe was under our dominion. Oh, a despot or two would occasionally take a swipe, but a bit of British spunk would soon see them running off with their tail between their legs. Whether they liked it or not, Johnny Foreigner learned a few manners and in return for letting us impose a couple of light taxes and half-inch a few family heirlooms they got railways, a firm but fair administration, democracy and cricket. If anything they did better out of the deal than we did.

But we had to go and let the hand-wringers bugger it all up, didn't we. Oh no, we couldn't be in someone else's country supplying a bit of education and law and order and taking them off the goat monetary system. Perish the thought. It's wrong. They have the right to self-determination and blah, blah, bloody blah. What about the right of conquest, eh? Never mind British pride and how His Majesty's going to feel when he finds out the namby-pambies are going to make Him hand India over to some skinny bloke in a pair of John Lennon specs and a loincloth. One day an Emperor of India, next day, 'Apologies George but if you look on the bright side there's still the Falklands,' as if ruling over a couple of penguins is going to make up for the loss of the jewel in the crown. So off we scuffle with a 'Sorry about that chaps but, look, keep the railways as a thank you present and we'll still meet up for cricket' and a couple of weeks later the British Empire on which the sun never set is replaced by a Commonwealth of Nations who all hate us and our standing in the international community is nil. Britain is the drunk old uncle at a wedding shouting, 'Ah used ta be *somebody*!'

With a blow to the national psyche, it's no wonder Britain's in the state it's in. From superpower to dirty old vagrant in a couple of generations. What a crying bloody shame.

The European Union

It all seemed like such a good idea at first, cosying up to our closest neighbours with a few preferential trade agreements. Where's the harm in that? Forgive and forget. We're all jolly good friends now, eh Pierre? But it's completely out of hand now, isn't it? I mean, for goodness sake, where's British sovereignty these days? I'm sure I just put it down over here a moment ago, but now we're being told what to do by some faceless gang of foreigners led by a moustachioed Romanian whose old mum hobbles about under a huge bundle of sticks and who probably couldn't even point to Britain on a map, let alone speak the Queen's English. Some mistake, surely?And as if that wasn't bad enough, the Germans are having a meddle too. The bloody Krauts. As if we didn't win the war; oh, sorry Wolfgang, strike that, we're all jolly good friends now, *Jawohl*?

There's huge assemblies of corrupt, non-elected Eurocrats in Brussels leaking billions of our money every year, but couldn't tell you where it's gone if their lives depended on it. Though chances are if you fished around in their sock drawers you might find more than a bit of loose change. And how do they justify their existence? By telling us we can't use Imperial measurements any more and how bendy a tomato should be; forcing constitutions or treaties or whatever it's called today on people who'd rather not ifyoudon'tmind thankyouverymuch; and letting in countries that aren't even properly in Europe. Where's the bloody logic? Is it called the Union of Backward Dirt Patches That Think They Might Be Able To Milk Some Taxpayers' Money Out Of Britain? No, it's bloody not. So sod off back to your yurt and get your hand out of my pocket.

Bloody hell, if it weren't for the Polish plumbers, I'd be voting UKIP. To my mind, if we've *got* to have a united Europe then you want to put one country in charge. A country that knows how to win a war or two. A country that's had a bit of experience in running a large empire. A country, perhaps, whose language is used predominantly throughout the western world …

The French

While I'm on the subject of Europe, let's take a closer look at our nearest neighbours, shall we? A peek under the sweat-stained duvet, so to speak. Now, you probably think I'm going to go on and on about eating snails and smelling of garlic and having a collective national bath phobia, etc. etc., but I'm not – even though all those things are true – because I'm a fair man and I realise that every nation has its own funny ways. I'm sure they find our great talent for pop music and ability to keep our hands to ourselves equally as baffling. No, what upsets me about the French is that they're all oddballs and cheaters. You can't tell me that a nation of adulterers who spend half their time wrapped in a tangle of dirty sheets with the neighbour's missus, puffing on a Gauloises with what appears to be a cowpat balanced on their head, is a nation of decent, trustworthy people. No, of course not.

They'd like us to think they've changed, of course. They send their short-arse president over to grovel to Her Majesty a bit and say thank you for keeping Charles de Gaulle out of their hair during the war, but behind our backs, when they think we can't hear, they call us 'Les Rosbifs' because we eat roast beef, the cheeky bloody Frogs. And of course the one thing Monsieur le Presidente doesn't bring up when meeting the Queen is the British Crown's perfectly legal claim to large swathes of Aquitaine and Normandy, which were taken off us under duress in the fifteenth century. That's next-door neighbours for you though I suppose. They probably said they just wanted to borrow them for a couple of days but would give them straight back, and have you got a cup of *sucre* and a spare *oeuf* while I'm here.

Eurovision

If you want to get a flavour of how the European Union's going to end up, you only have to look at the Eurovision Song Contest. What a bloody palaver. When I was a lad you had a handful of countries pitting their brightest talents against the rest of Europe in a sense of fun and fair play. Acts like Cliff Richard and Bucks Fizz. The chosen few representing all our great nations' hopes and dreams. Of course some poor beggar – usually Finland – was always going to end up with *nul points*, but only if their song was complete bobbins, and Britain was guaranteed a top-five placing.

Now what have you got? Hundreds of pitiful little eastern-bloc countries whose population must be stark, raving loony to field Vinkivitch and Vankovitch, two epileptics with their ode to 'Piff Paff Puff' or some gigantic bird warbling on about 'piss off all nations', like it was a bloody dirty song competition. But it doesn't matter that their 'entry' is about as enjoyable as root canal surgery, because they all block-vote for one another anyway. Everyone else knows it's a waste of time so they just send along some dolly bird wearing a piece of string and a belt so they can at least have a good ogle and oh, some tranny from Israel's turned up again, even though it was in the Middle East last time anyone looked. He/she comes every year though, so best humour him/her.

No one takes it seriously except Britain. Year after year we send in the best we have to offer. Fantastic acts such as that lot that did the song while dressed as flight attendants, and Andy who *almost* won *X-Factor*. It's no use though. BBC licence-payer's money is paying for everything, our technicians are showing everyone else how to wind up their clockwork cameras and Terry's there adding a bit of class to the proceedings, but we could put the Rolling Beatles on stage with Freddie Mercury on vocals and we'd still only get a couple of sympathy points from Ireland.

And that in microcosm is your European Union. It was our idea, we're paying for it and we've got all the talent, but the riff-raff have gatecrashed the party, nicked all the booze and are getting off with your girlfriend.

Accordions

In some ways we here in Great Britain don't know how lucky we are. And one of those ways is that we've totally escaped the accordion plague, thanks to the English Channel, no doubt. Because, let's face it, the worst thing – and it really does drive me up the bloody wall – about going abroad is that the minute you step off the bloody ferry all you can hear is bloody accordions. They *love* them. The French, the Germans, the Spanish, The Greek … you can be having a quiet drink anywhere across Euroland and the next thing you know some mousta-chioed old sadist has got the old squeezebox out and is sitting there swaying along to some crappy old folk tune written by an eighteenth-century chickenherd. In any civilised country this would be the cue for some caring member of the community to take him gently by the elbow and lead him out to the car park where he can do no more harm, but do the Europeans do the sensible thing? Oh no. They're clapping along. And dancing. To accordion music. Like he's Kylie Minogue.

In my humble opinion there is no more convincing argument that we're not, and never can be, a true part of Europe than the fact that we alone have not succumbed to this dreadful scourge.

Brits Abroad

If you were lucky enough to go on holiday somewhere exotic like Benidorm in the old days the sight of your fellow countrymen and women at play would make you proud. A jauntily positioned Panama hat, crisply ironed socks pulled up to the knees, a starched shirt and linen jacket with a pair of comfortable sandals. That was your average Brit. They might open a button or two on the beach while tucking in to Ian Fleming's latest and then it would be back to the hotel for a small gin and tonic and to put on a tie before hitting a quiet taverna to sample the local delicacies. All very civilised. It was enough to make the locals curse that they hadn't been born British.

Fast-forward fifty years and you'd think that the entire nation had been abducted by aliens. Where have they gone, these doughty British folk who always carried a Collins phrasebook in their pocket and would applaud a spot of Flamenco dancing politely before retiring for a game of whist and a cheeky Cinzano, because 'we *are* on holiday after all'? Sadly, they are with us no longer and instead we are represented abroad by a new breed of British holiday-makers. The unholy spawn of a lagered-up barbarian horde and a plague of locusts. Everywhere you go across the globe, beach communities will be infested with beer-gutted, screeching yobbos whose mission will be to get as pissed as possible and shag anything that stays still long enough. You can see them in hotel lobbies, drunkenly humping the pot plants with their pants round their ankles and strips of flesh peeling off like someone's taken a blow torch to them, because sun cream's for pansies. Come the morning they'll be throwing the Germans' towels in the pool and empty bottles at the natives. If you thought binge-drinking in Britain was bad just go and have a look at these buggers on holiday. At home they might be covered in sick and crawling around in the gutter, but that's just a quiet workday evening out. Once they get away from it all they can *really* relax and let their hair down. They're slinging the sangria and the ouzo and the tequila down their necks like the resort might run out any second, and God forbid you suggest they sample some of the local fare. Oh no. They've got to have their greasy eggs and bacon served in a bar with satellite TV if you please, because while they might be on holiday in foreignland they wouldn't want to miss what's happening in *EastEnders*, let alone a single game of football.

I blame the decline of Butlins. Well-kept secret at the time, but your basic holiday camp was a British conspiracy to keep all the riffraff locked up behind a wire fence for two weeks and away from anywhere they might embarrass the rest of us.

Foreign Waiters

I'm not saying that the foreigners are perfect either, mind. There's one or two in every country that could give Prince Philip a run for his money in a rudeness derby; a small minority that have the thuggish mentality of a Moss Side teenager and a sneer permanently plastered on their mugs. And there's one profession to which they are all drawn, like chavs to Smirnoff Ice: waiting tables.

Always a nation that likes to tick everyone else off, the French invented rude waiters single-handedly, and years later they can still field world-class table jockeys with a French Fry on every shoulder, top lips curled back so far it's like they're hanging off the ceiling by an invisible string, and an unmatched expertise in pouring a drop or two of red wine on your white shirt just where it shows. Oh yes, take a weekend break in Paris and you'll soon find the city's romantic ambience popped by some stony-faced, contrary git in tight trousers who'll ignore you for hours while he sharpens up his surliness. But of late they've slipped back in the running. The Spanish were the first to take offensive behaviour to a whole new level. Where your French waiter will be rude to anyone and everyone, without prejudice or favour, the Spanish perfected a technique that allows them to make any man that happens to be sitting at the table feel like an annoying insect while *simultaneously* subjecting his female companion to a disgusting display of oily Mediterranean smarm. You can try and order a paella, but you've got no chance whatsoever, because Diego is slowly rubbing himself against your missus, murmuring sweet nothings in her ear and gently undressing her at the table. Try and interrupt with a polite 'I say could you put my wife's breasts down for a moment and fetch me some calamari' and there's every chance he'll stab you with his biro.

The champions though, the undisputed worst waiters in the world ever, are the North Africans. Where even your French and Spanish waiters would be satisfied at the end of the meal to see a little bit of spare change left on the table, your Moroccan or Tunisian waiter will be looking for just a little bit more out of a tip. That's why you'll see doe-eyed nineteen-year-olds with eyelashes like Bambi and the figure of an Olympic swimmer, flocking around someone's Great Aunt Betty. Her old man's just passed on and she's got her legs bandaged up because the varicose veins are playing merry hell, but she's dragged herself away for a break in the sun and is now sat down for a cup of coffee and a bun. To everyone else she looks like a poorly old lady who's gone to seed a little bit, but to Ahmed the waiter she's a passport, an endless supply of money and a new life in a country where he doesn't have to work twenty-three hours a day in the boiling heat for tuppence a year. If he can just screw his eyes up at night for a couple of weeks and think of Tunisia he's going to be living like a king in exotic Hull.

Six weeks later Ahmed and Betty will be walking down the aisle under the aghast gaze of her relatives. Six weeks and one day later Ahmed will have moved into the spare room while he ticks off the days until he can apply for citizenship and he'll be draining Betty's bank account to move his extended family into the garage.

Oppression of Women

It beggars belief that there are countries in the world that get away with treating their women like second-hand citizens. You know the ones; where the ladies are locked in a room all day under a blanket with a couple of holes cut out. If they try and drive a car it's off to chokey with them. I mean, why do *they* get to treat women like that? I've tried it and, frankly, the results have not been pretty. I've explained time and time again to the wife that we should respect the cultural traditions of others so from now on she's to keep her gob shut, her hands off my motor and her sister has to wear a bag on her head if she comes round, but no; apparently I'm *oppressing* her. So I've told her what I've read from some Saudi Arabian lady in the *Guardian*, i.e. it's not oppression, it's *liberating*. She's freed up from all those mundane decisions like what to have for tea and whether I should be allowed another glass of Scotch. All she has to do is whatever I tell her and she'll discover a life of simple purity and spiritual fulfilment.

She won't have it though, which – if you ask me – is disrespectful of other people's folkways. Make that point though and from the way she glares at me you'd think *I* was the bigot.

The U S of A

Where do you bloody start with the yanks, eh? It all went wrong for them when the cheeky buggers started throwing tea around. Now, in my opinion that was a mistake. They weren't trying to start a revolution, they were trying to make the world's biggest cuppa in Boston Harbour. You know what they're like, they've got to have the biggest of everything. But being backwards colonials they didn't realise you need *hot* water, with sugar, not salt. Still, it was too late by then. Britain quite rightly took umbrage – after all you don't just go wasting good tea – and next thing you know we've decided they're more trouble than they're worth and left them to it. No, don't thank us for setting you up and letting you borrow our king, and don't bother to write.

And there it should have ended. We've got the hump with you so you stay on your side of the Atlantic with your Batmobile motors and your two thousand flavours of ice cream and we'll stay on ours with our tea-making know-how. But no, the bloody Yanks have got to have their revenge and pretty soon they've started shipping all their old rubbish over whether we wanted it or not. If they're not allowed to be British any more than dang if they ain't gonna turn us all into 'Yankee Doodle Dandy' whistling, grit 'n' gravy sucking yippee-ki-yays who can't even play rugby properly or grasp the rules of rounders.

It began with Hollywood movies. Now, in the old days we had a perfectly serviceable film industry of our own. Hardly anyone got shot, but what we lacked in gratuitous violence we made up for with the polished charm of your Terry Thomases and David Nivens. Many a fine British picture was made about a polite misunderstanding over a hat. After that it was the music. Oh, Harry Secombe put up a good fight with his lovely tenor voice and patriotic hymns, but suddenly everyone wants to listen to a deranged hillbilly kicking a piano. By now the floodgates have opened. Everyone's forgotten that America is just a tedious little colony that got a bit uppity and is sucking on milkshakes and calling each other 'daddio' and the rot's set in for good. The unique and wonderful British way of life that lasted for thousands of years, is over.

Suddenly you can't move for septics clogging up the nation's beauty spots and if you don't like *Friends* or *CSI* or *Jerry Springer* or the Simpsons or a ton of other old American bobbins then you might as well throw your TV away. Plus the British film industry's waving the white flag and a generation of teenagers are wearing baseball caps back to front and calling each other 'Holmes', but not in remembrance of the great detective. No, because it's what the bloody rappers do.

These days it's gotten to the point where you're almost relieved to see Noel Edmonds on the telly. He might be a git, but at least he's our git.

Peace on Earth

We almost managed it a couple of years ago. Apart from in Iraq and Afghanistan no one was fighting anyone. As close as we've ever been to Peace on Earth. Which makes me think; the only thing now stopping everyone getting on is a couple of rogue nations* and what's going on in

*Why do they call them 'rogue' nations? It's not as if they're some raffish little country with a cheeky smile and a twinkle in their eye, is it? 'Bastard' nations would seem more appropriate.

the bloody Middle East. And at the heart of *that* is this Israel–Palestine nonsense.

Now, I don't know about you, but I've had it up to here with Israel–Palestine. Every time I've opened the bloody paper for the last fifty years it's splashed all over. More lives lost, everyone's living in fear and the nutters are now using it as an excuse to try and blow up Exeter of all places. Well, luckily for the world I've sat and had a bit of a think about it over my Sultana Bran and have solved the problem. And this is how.

No one in the Middle East likes Israel. If Israel was at a party it would be edging towards the bedroom to get its coat. But *America* likes Israel, and America's got loads of space currently not being used for much. So what I want to know is if they can take London Bridge down and rebuild it in the United States, why can't they do the same with Israel? All right it might take a few weeks, unless you get a couple of boatloads of Polish builders on the job, but a few tankers full of carefully numbered bricks and hey presto; Israel's risen again in the middle of Iowa. The only people a bit put out are a couple of straw-chewing farmers, who've woken up to find a Wailing Wall where the Bottom Paddock used to be, but once you point out to them that they now own some prime real estate in the suburbs of Jerusalem and that their shopping opportunities have never been better I'm sure they'll be as pleased as punch.

Meanwhile the Palestinians have got their country back and Al-Qaida are suddenly looking a bit silly. No-one's got anything to argue about any more, we can all concentrate on sorting out those one or two pesky rogues and I'm just popping out to collect my Nobel Prize.

And that, in a nutshell, is the Grumpy Plan for lasting world peace. You're bloody welcome.